GREAT
WORD
HOUSE

MW00388586

LEVELS 1-4

An Orton-Gillingham
Reading & Spelling Program
35 Lesson Plans

For use with

My Book of Words 1
for Students

ISBN 978-1986424233
Printed in Toronto, Canada
Published and Distributed by:

PLOVER PRESS
PUBLISHING

TABLE OF CONTENTS

TABLE OF CONTENTS

Introduction

The Great Word House™ Spelling and Reading Program

Who Can Use the Program?

The GWH program is for all students aged 6 - 14 years who are studying the English language. These students may be in Kindergarten/Grade 1, they may be struggling readers and spellers, or they may be learning English as a second language (ESL).

How to Use the Program

The GWH™ program consists of four Teacher Guides and accompanying Student Booklets that progress from basic to advanced skills. In total there are 12 levels in the program. The books can be used on their own or in conjunction with lesson plans and supporting materials available from The Great Word House™ (GWH) online program.

The Teacher Guides have explicit instructions and the lesson plans are to be delivered in the sequence suggested. The skills taught are cumulative and each lesson may include skills taught in previous lessons.

Course Content Levels 1 - 4

The Scope and Sequence of GWH™ Levels 1 – 4 teaches alphabetic knowledge and 1-syllable words with *short* vowels. This first stage must be mastered to avoid later confusion with *long* vowel sounds. When the student learns to recognize the spelling patterns associated with *short* vowels in Closed Syllables then more complex patterns are taught. GWH™ shows how reading and spelling English can be broken down into predictable pattern recognition and mastered using our carefully structured lesson plans based on the Orton-Gillingham Approach.

Each level builds on previous levels taught and spirals back in reading and spelling dictation exercises to include lower level skills. Thus, review is built into every lesson.

Introduction

The Great Word House™ Spelling and Reading Program

Course Content Levels 1 - 4 Continued

High Frequency words that have irregular spelling patterns are taught from Level 1. These words are called *High Frequency* as they are the most frequently used words, occurring in the earliest sentences to be read and spelled. They are also referred to as *Sight Words* and need to be recognized automatically to promote reading fluency. *Sight Words* are not sounded out and taught by rote memorization.

Terminology

The Great Word House™ Spelling and Reading Program

Syllable

A **syllable** is a word or part of a word that has at least one vowel and may have consonants.

Closed Syllables

A syllable is a word or part of a word that has a vowel sound and a vowel letter. A syllable with a single vowel followed by one or more consonants is called a **Closed Syllable** and the vowel sound is *short*. **Closed Syllables** are the first syllables taught. The image of a closed door may help students remember the concept.

at   pot   egg   hitch

Open Syllables

When a syllable ends with 1 vowel and is not closed in by a consonant, it is an **Open Syllable**. The vowel sound is *long* and says its name. The first **Open Syllable** taught in Level 3 ends in vowel *y* which borrows from the sound and name of the letter *i*.

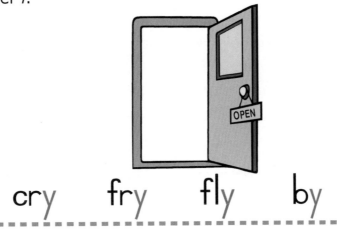

cry   fry   fly   by

GREAT WORD HOUSE
Reading & Spelling Program

Terminology

The Great Word House™ Spelling and Reading Program

Symbols

Sounds are written using / /

 above the vowel means the vowel sound is *short*

 above the vowel means the vowel sound is *long* or says its name

Sound Cues

 noisy – the sound vibrates the vocal cords or voice box

 quiet – the sound does not vibrate the vocal cords

Do not add "uh" when saying the sound for quiet letters as this makes the sound noisy and is an incorrect pronunciation.

Vowels

A **vowel** is a noisy stream of unblocked air. Every word must have a vowel. Some words are only vowels, e.g. *I*, *a*. The vowel letters are **a**, **e**, **i**, **o**, **u**. **y** is a vowel when it occurs in the middle or end of words. *y* sounds like *long i*, e.g. *fly*. Later, students learn that *y* also borrows the *long e* and *short i* sound.

Consonants

Consonants can be quiet and noisy with the lips, teeth and tongue blocking the air. Consonants differ from vowels because the air is blocked to some degree, they do not say their names and alone they cannot form syllables.

Terminology

The Great Word House™ Spelling and Reading Program

Digraphs

A **digraph** refers to two letters that make one sound. Two consonants that make one sound are called consonant digraphs. Later, students learn that two vowels can make one sound and are called vowel digraphs or vowel teams.

Clusters

A **cluster** refers to two or more letters that commonly occur together, e.g. *sl-* in initial position and *-nd* in final position. Each letter in a cluster can be heard. Digraphs can be part of clusters, e.g. *thr-*.

Teaching the Alphabet & First Words with Short Vowels

Levels 1 - 4 of the Scope and Sequence teaches the foundation of alphabetic knowledge and 1-syllable words with short vowels. This stage must be mastered in order to build subsequent concepts and skills. Consolidation and mastery may take weeks or months. Even when advancing to subsequent levels, spiral back and review concepts taught in Levels 1 – 4.

Levels 1 - 2				
Closed Syllables	**Word**			
VC	on	at	up	
CVC	cat	bet	sun	
CCVC Digraphs	shin	chop	this	
CVCC Digraphs	math	duck	fish	
Spelling Rule				
FF-LL-SS-ZZ	huff	pill	bass	fuzz
Suffixes				
-s	bats	dogs		
-es	buzzes	glasses		

Level 3		
Open & Closed Syllable	**Word**	
CCV (y as vowel)	cry	fly
CCVC Clusters	clap	skid

Legend	
V	Vowel
C	Consonant

Overview
LEVELS 1 – 4
(continued)

Level 4			
Closed Syllable	**Word**		
VCC	and	apt	ask
CVCC	cost	sent	hulk
CVCCC	bench	winch	
CVCCe* (see below)	lunge	prince	
CCVCC Digraphs & Clusters	stash	thump	chant
Spelling Rule			
111 Doubling Rule	netting	chatted	shutting
Silent e (1st job)*	hinge	dance	
Drop the Silent e	hinging	dancing	
Suffixes			
-ed	filled	licked	landed
-ing	sending	batting	dancing

Legend	
V	Vowel
C	Consonant

111

11111111

Alphabet Drill Cards

Letters	Keywords	Sounds
a	apple	/ă/
b	boy	/b/
c	cat	/k/
d	dog	/d/
e	egg	/ĕ/
f	fish	/f/
g	goat	/g/
h	hat	/h/
i	itch	/ĭ/
j	jam	/j/
k	kite	/k/
l	lamp	/l/
m	man	/m/
n	net	/n/
o	octopus	/ŏ/
p	pot	/p/
qu	queen	/kw/
r	rat	/r/
s	snake	/s/
s_2	nose	/z/
t	top	/t/
u	up	/ŭ/
v	van	/v/
w	wind	/w/
x	box	/ks/
y (consonant)	yellow	/y/
y (vowel)	fly	/ī/
z	zebra	/z/
ch	church	/ch/
sh	ship	/sh/
th	thumb	/th/
th_2	there	/th̲/
-ck	duck	/k/

Alphabet Drill Cards By Level

Level 1

Letters:	a	c	d	f	g	l	m	n	o	p	t		
Noisy:	a		d		g	l	m	n	o				
Quiet:	c		f		p		t						

Level 2

Letters:	b	e	h	i	j	k	qu	r	s	s_2	u	v	w	x	y	z
Digraphs:	ch	sh	th	th_2	-ck											
Noisy:	b	e	i	j	k	r	s_2	u	v	w	y	z	th_2			
Quiet:	h	k	q	s	x	ch	sh	th	-ck							
Noisy + Quiet:	qu															

Level 3

Letters:	y (vowel)
Noisy:	y
Quiet:	

Level 4

Letters:	c_2	g_2	n_2
Digraphs:	wh	ng	
Word Family:	all		
1st Job Silent e:	dan**ce**	hin**ge**	
Noisy:	g_2	n_2	ng	wh
Quiet:	c_2		

Lesson Plan Elements

The lesson plan consists of six elements. Each element is built on the **Alphabet Card Drill**, which anchors the lesson plan. The **Alphabet Card Drill** is also referred to as the **Visual Auditory Kinesthetic/Tactile (VAKT) Drill**.

Present the elements in this order:

1. ALPHABET CARD DRILL

The drill teaches the students to remember the name of the letter and the sound it makes.

2. BLENDING

Students blend letter-sounds learned in the **Alphabet Card Drill** to read 1-syllable words. This is an optional step.

3. READING WORDS

Students practice rapid recognition of words, including **Sight Words**.

4. READING PHRASES/SENTENCES/PASSAGES

Students read words in context.

5. SPELLING WORDS

Students learn the procedure for segmenting a word into sounds. Students recall the letters associated with the sounds and spell the word. Students spell **Sight Words**.

6. PHRASE AND/OR SENTENCE DICTATION

Students write a phrase or sentence dictated by the teacher.

1. ALPHABET CARD DRILL

Use the **Alphabet Card Drill** to teach the student the name of the letter and the sound the letter makes. The keyword is not to be spelled. The keyword begins with the sound to be learned and helps the student link the letter name to its sound.

The **Alphabet Card Drill** has two parts.

The first part teaches the student to read. The student learns the name of the letter and the sound the letter makes. The student writes or traces the letter while saying the letter name, the keyword and the sound.

The second part teaches the student to spell. The student hears the sound, says the letter name, keyword, and writes or traces the letter(s).

LEARNING TO READ USING THE ALPHABET DRILL CARDS

The student looks at the **Alphabet Card**.

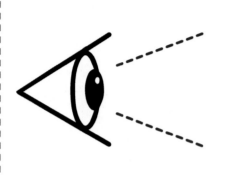

The teacher asks:

1. *What is the name of the letter?*

2. *What is the keyword?*

3. *What sound does this letter make?*

Use the **Lesson Plan Template** found in the **Appendix** and have the student write the letter saying the name of the letter, keyword and the sound. The students can trace the letters on a rough surface instead of writing the letters.

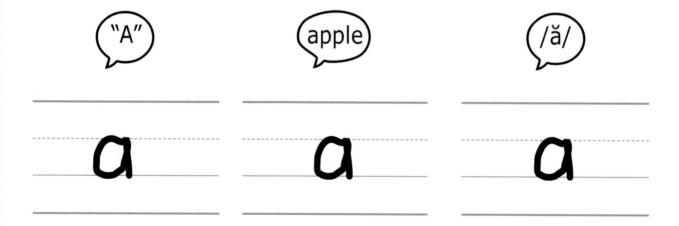

"A"   apple   /ă/

a   a   a

If the students have difficulty recalling the sound, tell them to hold the first sound of the keyword.

"A"   aaaaaaaaapple   /ă/

LEARNING TO SPELL USING THE ALPHABET DRILL CARDS

In this part of the **Alphabet Drill**, the students do not see the card. They hear the sound and need to recall the letter associated with the sound.

For example,

The teacher asks: *What spells the sound /ă/?*

The student writes the letter three times while saying:

"A"   apple   /ă/

a   a   a

If the students have difficulty recalling letter formation, name or keyword, show them the letter and ask them to trace or write over it. Moving the hand or fingers in a familiar path may trigger recall. The teacher can also show a picture of the keyword.

LESSON PLAN ELEMENTS

2. BLENDING

Using the drill cards in the **Alphabet Card Drill**, create vowel-consonant (VC) combinations for the student to blend. The student says the sound of each letter and blends to form a syllable. Sometimes the syllable will be a real word and sometimes a nonsense word. The teacher should point out the nonsense words, so no confusion arises.

Start with consonant sounds that are easier to hold, like **m** and **n**.

Vowel Consonant Word Families (VC)

a	m		o	m
a	n		o	n
a	d		o	d
a	g		o	g
a	p		o	p
a	t		o	t

LESSON PLAN ELEMENTS

3. READING WORDS

When the student can blend letters into syllables, print the words on cards or in a list. Students need to practice quick and efficient word recognition. Group words by **Word Family**, vowel or put into alphabetical order. Teach the students meanings and parts of speech.

4. READING OF PHRASES, SENTENCES AND PASSAGES

The student reads words based on the **Alphabet Card Drill** in context, so that meaning and usage of the words can be learned. **Sight Words** occurring in these phrases, sentences and passage need to be taught.

5. SPELLING WORDS

Spelling words has five steps. The teacher dictates a word and the student:
- Says the word the back to ensure that it has been heard correctly.
- Segments the word into sounds.
- Gives the letter names.
- Writes the word saying the letter names.
- Reads the word back.

6. PHRASE AND/OR SENTENCE DICTATION

The teacher dictates a phrase or sentence.
The student repeats the phrase or sentence back to the teacher to ensure it has been heard correctly.
The student writes the sentence in the **Sentence Dictation Template** found in the **Appendix** or a notebook. The template has prompts for a **capital** and a **period**.

Capital   **Period**

EXAMPLE #1 LESSON PLAN FOR LEVEL 1
Short Vowels *a*, *o* in CVC Words
Using Word Families

1. ALPHABET CARD DRILL

Reading Drill

Show the student one **Alphabet Drill Card** at a time. The student writes/traces the letter saying the letter(s) name(s), keyword and sound.

Use **Teacher Prompts** if necessary.

What is the name of this letter?

What is the keyword?

What is the sound this letter makes?

a	c	d	f	g	l
m	n	o	p	t	

Spelling Drill

Do not show student each **Alphabet Drill Card** and ask:

What letter spells the sounds?

The teacher says the sound and the student traces/writes the letter(s) while saying the letter name(s), keyword and sound.

/ă/	/k/	/d/	/f/	/g/	/l/
/m/	/n/	/ŏ/	/p/	/t/	

2. BLENDING

Student says the sounds of each letter and blends to form a syllable.

Vowel Consonant Word Families (VC)

a	m		o	m
a	n		o	n
a	d		o	d
a	g		o	g
a	p		o	p
a	t		o	t

EXAMPLE #1 LESSON PLAN FOR LEVEL 1
Short Vowels *a*, *o* in CVC Words
Using Word Families

3. WORD READING

Add a consonant in front of the **Word Family** to form **CVC words**.

Student says: *If I can read* **am** *then I can read* **cam, dam, lam, Pam**

Student says: *If I can read* **an** *then I can read* **can**, **Dan**, **fan**, **pan**, **tan**

Student says: *If I can read* **ag** *then I can read* **lag**, **mag**, **nag**, **tag**

Student says: *If I can read* **ap** *then I can read* **cap**, **gap**, **lap**, **map**, **nap**

Student says: *If I can read* **ot** *then I can read* **dot**, **got**, **lot**, **not**, **pot**

Student says: *If I can read* **od** *then I can read* **cod**, **god**, **mod**, **nod**, **pod**

SIGHT WORDS:

a	of	the

4. PHRASE/SENTENCE READING

fan on

mad lad

fat cat

not cod

on the lam

dog on a log

Student reads sentences and needs to know **Sight Words**, capitals and punctuation.

The lad can fan the cat.

The man got a lot of cod.

A cat got mad at a dog.

Nat can fan dad.

Pat the dog, Pam!

5. SPELLING WORDS

Ask the student to spell 5 - 10 words they read.

Example,

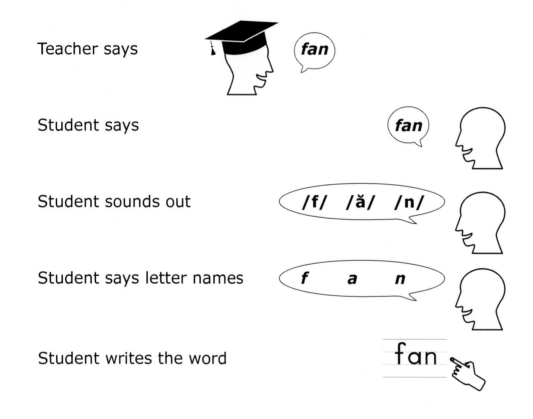

Teacher says	*fan*
Student says	*fan*
Student sounds out	/f/ /ă/ /n/
Student says letter names	f a n
Student writes the word	fan

fan	dam	can	dad	tag
pot	cod	not	got	fog

6. PHRASE OR SENTENCE DICTATION

fat cat

fan on

mad lad

fat cat

not cod

on the lam

dog on a log

The student needs to spell **Sight Words**, and be able to use capitals and periods. Use **Sentence Dictation** template in the **Appendix** or once the students have written the sentence, ask them to highlight the capital and place a red dot on the period.

The lad got mad.

The man got a tan.

Nat can fan dad.

Pam got mad.

Dan can nap on a log.

The mad lad ran to the dam.

EXAMPLE #2 LESSON PLAN FOR LEVEL 1
Short Vowels *a*, *o* in CVC Words

Student/Class: Date: Lesson #:

1. ALPHABET CARD DRILL

  Reading Drill

Show the student one **Alphabet Drill Card** at a time. The student writes/ traces the letter saying the letter(s) name(s), keyword and sound.

Use **Teacher Prompts** if necessary.

What is the name of this letter?

What is the keyword?

What is the sound this letter makes?

a	c	d	f	g	l
m	n	o	p	t	

Spelling Drill

Do not show student each **Alphabet Drill Card** and ask:

What letter spells the sounds?

The teacher says the sound and the student traces/writes the letter(s)while saying the letter name(s), keyword and sound.

/ă/	/k/	/d/	/f/	/g/	/l/
/m/	/n/	/ŏ/	/p/	/t/	

2. BLENDING

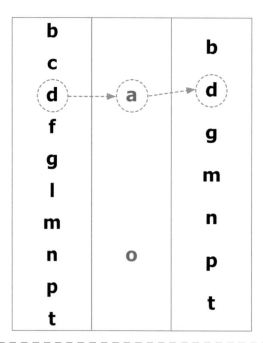

EXAMPLE #2 LESSON PLAN FOR LEVEL 1
Short Vowels *a*, *o* in CVC Words

3. WORD READING

top	fad	pot	lad	Tom
mat	dog	pal	log	cop
lop	lad	pat	lag	at
pan	pod	gag	gap	nag
tap	on	map	nap	pop
cod	mom	can	fat	tag
dad	mog	got	an	not
lap	tan	Nat	Pam	cap

SIGHT WORDS:

a	the	

4. SENTENCE READING

Nat got a dog.

Tap the cat.

Pot the cod.

Map the dam.

Pat the dog.

The dog can tag the cat.

The lad can nap on the mat.

Tom got a pop can.

The cat can nap.

A lad got mad.

EXAMPLE #2 LESSON PLAN FOR LEVEL 1
Short Vowels *a*, *o* in CVC Words

5. SPELLING WORDS

tag	lot	fog	dog	cat
mom	pop	gag	pan	fat

6. SENTENCE DICTATION

Nat got a dog.

Tap the cat.

Pot the cod.

Map the dam.

Pat the dog.

EXAMPLE #3 LESSON PLAN FOR LEVEL 2
Short Vowels *a, e, o* in CVC Words

Student/Class: Date: Lesson #:

1. ALPHABET CARD DRILL

 Reading Drill

Show the student one **Alphabet Drill Card** at a time. The student writes/ traces the letter saying the letter(s) name(s), keyword and sound.

Use **Teacher Prompts** if necessary.

What is the name of this letter?

What is the keyword?

What is the sound this letter makes?

a	b	c	d	e	f
g	h	j	l	m	n
o	p	r	s	t	

Spelling Drill

Do not show student each **Alphabet Drill Card** and ask:

What letter spells the sounds?

The teacher says the sound and the student traces/writes the letter(s)while saying the letter name(s), keyword and sound.

/ă/	/b/	/k/	/d/	/ě/	/f/
/g/	/h/	/j/	/l/	/m/	/n/
/ŏ/	/p/	/r/	/s/	/t/	

2. BLENDING

b		b		b
c		d		d
d	a	g	m	a	g
f	e	m	n	e	m
g	o	n	p	o	n
h		p	r		p
j		t	s		t
l			t		

EXAMPLE #3 LESSON PLAN FOR LEVEL 2
Short Vowels _a_, _e_, _o_ in CVC Words

3. WORD READING

bet	fad	bed	lad	top
mat	dog	pal	pat	hot
rod	lot	pet	lag	Meg
ran	pen	bat	gap	peg
top	hem	job	tap	ham
jab	map	not	rat	nap
rag	Jan	den	can	jog
fat	pod	tag	fog	sad
cab	met	rot	Sam	bag

SIGHT WORDS:

a	the	to

4. SENTENCE READING

The dog can jog at the dam.

The cat had a wet leg.

A sad pet sat on the mat.

A hen fed on a cob.

Meg ran to bed.

Sam got a cab to the job.

The lad sat on a log.

Dad has a red bat.

The rat got a lot of jam.

Ted let Dot nab the cab.

EXAMPLE #3 LESSON PLAN FOR LEVEL 2
Short Vowels *a*, *e*, *o* in CVC Words

5. SPELLING WORDS

let	met	cab	job	sob
lag	tap	hot	pen	men

6. SENTENCE DICTATION

The man had a red cab.

Ted fed a hen at the dam.

Bob has not got a map.

The cat ran on the log.

Sam sat on top of the hog.

GREAT WORD HOUSE ™
Reading & Spelling Program

Student/Class: **Date:**   **Lesson #:**

---

1. ALPHABET CARD DRILL

 Reading Drill

Show the student one **Alphabet Drill Card** at a time. The student writes/traces the letter saying the letter(s) name(s), keyword and sound.

Use **Teacher Prompts** if necessary.

What is the name of this letter?

What is the keyword?

What is the sound this letter makes?

a	b	c	d	e	f
g	h	i	j	l	m
n	o	p	r	s	t
v	w	y	z		

 Spelling Drill

Do not show student each **Alphabet Drill Card** and ask:

What letter spells the sounds?

The teacher says the sound and the student traces/writes the letter(s) while saying the letter name(s), keyword and sound.

/ă/	/b/	/k/	/d/	/ě/	/f/
/g/	/h/	/ĭ/	/j/	/l/	/m/
/n/	/ŏ/	/p/	/r/	/s/	/t/
/v/	/w/	/y/	/z/		

EXAMPLE #4 LESSON PLAN FOR LEVEL 2
Short Vowels *a*, *e*, *i*, *o* in CVC Words, no *k*, *qu* and *x*

2. BLENDING

b		
c		b
d		
f		d
g	a	
h		g
j	e	
l	i	m
v	o	
w		n
y		p
z		t

3. WORD READING

fat	bag	bid	rot	sat
hot	get	pip	cob	hit
red	lad	pit	sob	got
rob	pen	bat	dab	pig
tip	mom	jab	pin	yam
pot	rat	not	bet	pod
bog	log	Dan	rag	jog
cop	Ben	pop	fit	cod
den	pal	lap	fin	dog
wig	sip	zip	lap	wit

SIGHT WORDS:

a	and	of
the		

4. SENTENCE READING

The pig can not fit in the pen.

The cat had a big nap on the mat.

Get a rag and dab his wet leg.

A cab hit a log in the fog.

The dog can dig in the bog.

Dan got in a red cab.

Sam is a big lad.

Pat met Meg at the dam.

The log has a lot of rot.

Ted had a yam and a hot cob.

5. SPELLING WORDS

pig	wig	lid	zip	yam
yet	den	wet	jog	cod

6. SENTENCE DICTATION

The men had a lot of cod.

The hen hid in the pit.

A pig had a bit of cob.

Ted the rat had a nap in the fog.

Rob met Sam in a red cab.

EXAMPLE #5 LESSON PLAN FOR LEVEL 2
Short Vowels *a*, *e*, *o*, *u* in CVC Words, no *k*, *qu* and *x*

Student/Class: Date: Lesson #:

1. ALPHABET CARD DRILL

 Reading Drill

Show the student one **Alphabet Drill Card** at a time. The student writes/ traces the letter saying the letter(s) name(s), keyword and sound.

Use **Teacher Prompts** if necessary.

What is the name of this letter?

What is the keyword?

What is the sound this letter makes?

a	b	c	d	e	f
g	h	j	l	m	n
o	p	r	s	t	u
v	w	y	z		

Spelling Drill

Do not show student each **Alphabet Drill Card** and ask:

What letter spells the sounds?

The teacher says the sound and the student traces/writes the letter(s)while saying the letter name(s), keyword and sound.

/ă/	/b/	/k/	/d/	/ĕ/	/f/
/g/	/h/	/j/	/l/	/m/	/n/
/ŏ/	/p/	/r/	/s/	/t/	/ŭ/
/v/	/w/	/y/	/z/		

EXAMPLE #5 LESSON PLAN FOR LEVEL 2
Short Vowels *a*, *e*, *o*, *u* in CVC Words,
no *k*, *qu* and *x*

2. BLENDING

b c d f g h j l v w y z	a e o u	b d g m n p t

3. WORD READING

fat	bag	top	rum	sat
hut	get	pot	gun	hot
red	lad	fog	sun	mug
run	pen	bat	dab	lot
dot	hum	jab	job	yam
sup	rat	nut	bet	bun
nub	lug	Dan	dug	jug
cup	Ben	pug	nod	but
den	pal	lap	lot	fun
sob	rub	tum	lap	sum
men	yap	yum	zap	cub

SIGHT WORDS:

a	and	of
the	to	

EXAMPLE #5 LESSON PLAN FOR LEVEL 2
Short Vowels *a*, *e*, *o*, *u* in CVC Words, no *k*, *qu* and *x*

4. SENTENCE READING

The mat had a lot of mud.

The pug can nab the fat cat.

The lad had ham on a bun.

Sam had a fun job.

Ken had to lug a log to the hut.

Pam had a cup of pop.

Ben had run a lot and got hot.

Meg had a bag on the bed.

A red tug can lug a lot of cod.

Ted had a yam and a hot cob.

5. SPELLING WORDS

rub	cub	set	hem	wet
nut	bag	wag	top	lot

6. SENTENCE DICTATION

The cub had fun at the dam.

A bad cat got the cod.

The mat had a lot of mud.

Ted can hum and run.

A hen had a red tum.

EXAMPLE #6 LESSON PLAN FOR LEVEL 2
Short Vowels *a*, *e*, *i*, *o*, *u* in CVC Words, no *k*, *qu* and *x*

Student/Class: Date: Lesson #:

1. ALPHABET CARD DRILL

 Reading Drill

Show the student one **Alphabet Drill Card** at a time. The student writes/ traces the letter saying the letter(s) name(s), keyword and sound.

Use **Teacher Prompts** if necessary.

What is the name of this letter?

What is the keyword?

What is the sound this letter makes?

a	b	c	d	e	f
g	h	i	j	l	m
n	o	p	r	s	t
u	v	w	y	z	

 Spelling Drill

Do not show student each **Alphabet Drill Card** and ask:

What letter spells the sounds?

The teacher says the sound and the student traces/writes the letter(s)while saying the letter name(s), keyword and sound.

/ă/	/b/	/k/	/d/	/ĕ/	/f/
/g/	/h/	/ĭ/	/j/	/l/	/m/
/n/	/ŏ/	/p/	/r/	/s/	/t/
/ŭ/	/v/	/w/	/y/	/z/	

EXAMPLE #6 LESSON PLAN FOR LEVEL 2
Short Vowels *a*, *e*, *i*, *o*, *u* in CVC Words, no *k*, *qu* and *x*

2. BLENDING

b c d f g h j l v w y z	a e i o u	b d g m n p t

3. WORD READING

fit	jig	bud	rum	sat	bog
hut	get	pup	gun	hat	let
red	lad	pit	sun	mog	fig
run	pen	fog	dab	pig	pop
tip	hum	jab	pen	yam	tip
sup	rat	nut	bet	bun	get
nib	log	got	dug	jug	dig
cup	fen	pug	fat	but	nod
hog	did	rod	him	fan	pin
tip	tug	wag	zip	wit	zap
dam	men	yap	yum	zap	cub

SIGHT WORDS:

a	and	I
of	the	to

EXAMPLE #6 LESSON PLAN FOR LEVEL 2
Short Vowels *a*, *e*, *i*, *o*, *u* in CVC Words, no *k*, *qu* and *x*

4. SENTENCE READING

I can jab the nib in the can.

Did the pug lug the log to the hut?

The lad had a big red mug.

I had fun on the tug.

Can the man get a fan?

Pam can not dig in the hot sun.

Len got a fat hog in the pen.

Pin up the hem.

The wig had a dot of mud on it.

A hen can sup on a nut.

5. SPELLING WORDS

lit	hem	sun	zap	fog
wig	pen	bun	ram	got

6. SENTENCE DICTATION

Zap the bug.

The wig got mud on it.

A ram had a nap in the sun.

Ben can sup on a bun.

A lad lit a log in the fog.

EXAMPLE #7 LESSON PLAN FOR LEVEL 2
Short Vowels *a*, *e*, *i*, *o*, *u* in CVC Words, Introducing *k*

Student/Class:	Date:	Lesson #:

NEW CONCEPT: Always use c for /k/ at the beginning of a word except when followed by e and i then use k.

k is the go to guy for **e** and **i**.

1. ALPHABET CARD DRILL

 Reading Drill

Show the student one **Alphabet Drill Card** at a time. The student writes/traces the letter saying the letter(s) name(s), keyword and sound.

Use **Teacher Prompts** if necessary.

What is the name of this letter?

What is the keyword?

What is the sound this letter makes?

a	b	c	d	e	f
g	h	i	j	k	l
m	n	o	p	r	s
t	u	v	w	y	z

Spelling Drill

Do not show student each **Alphabet Drill Card** and ask:

What letter spells the sounds?

The teacher says the sound and the student traces/writes the letter(s)while saying the letter name(s), keyword and sound.

For Multiple Spellings Teacher Asks	Student Answers
How many ways can you spell /k/?	*c, k*

/ă/	/b/	/k/	/d/	/ĕ/	/f/
/g/	/h/	/ĭ/	/j/	/l/	/m/
/n/	/ŏ/	/p/	/r/	/s/	/t/
/ŭ/	/v/	/w/	/y/	/z/	

EXAMPLE #7 LESSON PLAN FOR LEVEL 2
Short Vowels *a*, *e*, *i*, *o*, *u* in CVC Words, Introducing *k*

2. BLENDING

c	a	b
k	e	d
	i	g
	o	m
	u	n
		p
		t

3. WORD READING

fit	jig	cud	rum	sat	bog
con	cop	pup	gun	cat	let
red	kid	kit	sun	mog	fig
run	pen	fog	dab	pig	pop
tip	hum	jab	Ken	yam	kip
sup	rat	nut	bet	cut	get
keg	log	got	dug	jug	dig
cup	kid	pug	fat	but	nod
cog	did	rod	cud	fan	pin
tip	tug	wag	kip	wit	zap
dam	kin	yap	cap	zap	cub

SIGHT WORDS:

a	and	I
of	the	to

EXAMPLE #7 LESSON PLAN FOR LEVEL 2
Short Vowels *a*, *e*, *i*, *o*, *u* in CVC Words, Introducing *k*

4. SENTENCE READING

The kid and the cub had fun.

Did the cat cut the ham?

The cup had a big red dot.

Ken got a big kit bag.

Can Kim dig in the fog?

The cop had a big hat.

Ten men got in the cab.

I can nap and I can kip.

The cat got a bit of cod.

The kid had a cog and a nut.

5. SPELLING WORDS

kit	kin	kid	ken	keg
cog	cup	cub	can	cab

6. SENTENCE DICTATION

Kim had a cup in the kit.

The cop had a cup of pop.

A red cab did ram the van.

Did Ken cut the bun?

A cub and a kid ran to the hut.

EXAMPLE #8 LESSON PLAN FOR LEVEL 2
Short Vowels *a, e, i, o, u* in CVC Words, Introducing *x*

Student/Class:　　　　　Date:　　　　　Lesson #:

NEW CONCEPT: x makes two sounds /ks/. x comes at the end of a word.
(Later teach that it is found in the middle of a word)

1. ALPHABET CARD DRILL

 Reading Drill

Show the student one **Alphabet Drill Card** at a time. The student writes/ traces the letter saying the letter(s) name(s), keyword and sound.

Use **Teacher Prompts** if necessary.

What is the name of this letter?

What is the keyword?

What is the sound this letter makes?

a	b	c	d	e	f
g	h	i	j	k	l
m	n	o	p	r	s
t	u	v	w	x	y
z					

 Spelling Drill

Do not show student each **Alphabet Drill Card** and ask:

What letter spells the sounds?

The teacher says the sound and the student traces/writes the letter(s)while saying the letter name(s), keyword and sound.

For Multiple Spellings Teacher Asks	Student Answers
How many ways can you spell /k/?	*c, k*

/ă/	/b/	/k/	/d/	/ĕ/	/f/
/g/	/h/	/ĭ/	/j/	/l/	/m/
/n/	/ŏ/	/p/	/r/	/s/	/t/
/ŭ/	/v/	/w/	/ks/	/y/	/z/

EXAMPLE #8 LESSON PLAN FOR LEVEL 2
Short Vowels *a*, *e*, *i*, *o*, *u* in CVC Words, Introducing *x*

2. BLENDING

b f h l m n p s t w	a e o u	x

3. WORD READING

fix	Rex	cud	rum	six	box
con	cop	pup	gun	sax	let
red	kid	kit	sun	mog	fig
lax	pen	fox	fax	pig	nix
tip	hum	jab	Ken	yam	kip
sup	rat	nut	bet	cut	hex
keg	lox	got	pox	jug	dig
cup	kid	tux	fat	but	nod
lox	did	rod	cud	tax	pin
tip	lux	wag	kip	mix	Max
dam	kin	yap	wax	zap	vex

SIGHT WORDS:

a	and	I
of	the	to

EXAMPLE #8 LESSON PLAN FOR LEVEL 2
Short Vowels *a*, *e*, *i*, *o*, *u* in CVC Words, Introducing *x*

4. SENTENCE READING

The box had a dot of wax on it.

Did the fox nab the hog?

Max had lox on a bun.

Ken had six men in the van.

The bat had a big tax on it.

The dog Rex dug a pit.

A pig had the pox.

Dan sat the sax in a box.

Max can fix the fax.

Dab the mix on the cod.

5. SPELLING WORDS

fix	mix	box	fox	hex
vex	tux	max	tax	six

6. SENTENCE DICTATION

The box had a lot of lox.

A red fox ran in the fen.

The cab had six men.

Did Rex mix up the cod and lox?

The cat can vex the rat.

EXAMPLE #9 LESSON PLAN FOR LEVEL 2
All Short Vowels in CVC Words,
Introducing a Suffix: Noisy and Quiet *-s*

Student/Class: **Date:**   **Lesson #:**

NEW CONCEPT: Some letters make two sounds, that is, they have more than one phoneme pronunciation. *s* can be a quiet letter and sounds like /s/. When *s* is next to noisy letters in the middle or at the end of a word, it can become noisy and sound like /z/. This is the second sound of *s* (s_2). Quiet letters are also called 'unvoiced' and noisy letters are called 'voiced'.

NEW CONCEPT: A suffix is added to the end of a word. The suffix *−s* comes at the end of the word. The hyphen indicates the point of attachment to the word. Suffix *-s* has two jobs:

1. *−s* makes nouns plural, e.g. *dogs*, *cats*.

2. *−s* is used with 3rd person singular verbs in the present tense or he/she/it verbs: *He nods. She sits. It naps.* You can use a proper or common noun instead of he/she/it: *Tom nods. Pam sits. A cat naps.*

1. ALPHABET CARD DRILL

 Reading Drill

Show the student one **Alphabet Drill Card** at a time. The student writes/traces the letter saying the letter(s) name(s), keyword and sound.
Use **Teacher Prompts** if necessary.

What is the name of this letter?

What is the keyword?

What is the sound this letter makes?

For Multiple Spellings Teacher Asks	Student Answers
What are the two sounds s makes?	*s snake /s/, s nose /z/*

a	b	c	d	e	f
g	h	i	j	k	l
m	n	o	p	r	s and s$_2$
t	u	v	w	x	y
z					

EXAMPLE #9 LESSON PLAN FOR LEVEL 2
All Short Vowels in CVC Words,
Introducing a Suffix: Noisy and Quiet -s

 Spelling Drill

Do not show student each **Alphabet Drill Card** and ask:

What letter spells the sounds?

The teacher says the sound and the student traces/writes the letter(s)while saying the letter name(s), keyword and sound.

For Multiple Spellings Teacher Asks	Student Answers
How many ways can you spell /k/?	c, k
How many ways can you spell /z/?	s, z

/ă/	/b/	/k/	/d/	/ĕ/	/f/
/g/	/h/	/ĭ/	/j/	/l/	/m/
/n/	/ŏ/	/p/	/r/	/s/	/t/
/ŭ/	/v/	/w/	/ks/	/y/	/z/

Suffix Drill

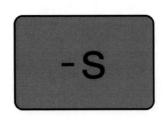

After the **Alphabet Card Drill**, tell the student that suffixes come at the end and are on red cards (red for 'stop'). The hyphen shows where the suffix is fixed or joined to the word.

Show the student the card and ask:

How do we know this is a suffix card? Answer: *It is red and the letter has a hyphen in front.*

What does this hyphen show? Answer: *Where the word joins to it.*

Please read the card. Answer: *Suffix −s says /s/ and /z/.*

What are the jobs of suffix −s? Answer: *It shows plural (more than one) e.g. cats, dogs. Suffix -s is used with he/she/it verbs, e.g. He digs. She digs. It digs. Proper and common nouns can be used instead of he/she/it.*

EXAMPLE #9 LESSON PLAN FOR LEVEL 2
All Short Vowels in CVC Words,
Introducing a Suffix: Noisy and Quiet *-s*

2. BLENDING

Look at the last letter in the word. If it is noisy, choose –s/z/. If it is quiet, choose –s/s/.

cat	
dog	
pot	
pug	-s /s/
top	
tip	
bet	
nut	
van	-s /z/
cab	
fig	
bat	

2. BLENDING Continued

Add suffix –s to make nouns plural

Singular Noun	Plural (more than 1)
a mat	2 _____
a map	4 _____
a mug	4 _____
a cop	5 _____
a ham	4 _____
a cat	3 _____
a tip	8 _____
a nut	9 _____
a van	2 _____

Add suffix –s to verbs in 3rd Person

I run.	It _____.
I sit.	She _____.
I nap.	The cat _____.
I wed.	She _____.
I tap.	Pam _____.
I hum.	He _____.
I bet.	Kim _____.
I dig.	Tim _____.
I jab.	It _____.

EXAMPLE #9 LESSON PLAN FOR LEVEL 2
All Short Vowels in CVC Words,
Introducing a Suffix: Noisy and Quiet -s

3. WORD READING

is	has	as	his	sits	hums
cons	cops	pups	guns	cats	lets
beds	kids	kits	suns	logs	figs
runs	pens	fogs	dabs	pigs	pops
tips	sums	jabs	tens	yams	kips
sups	rats	nuts	bets	cups	gets
wigs	legs	hems	dims	jugs	dogs
lips	lids	tugs	mats	huts	nods
cogs	dons	rods	pets	fans	pins
tans	pads	wags	digs	wits	zaps

SIGHT WORDS:

a	and	I
of	the	to

4. SENTENCE READING

The kids and the cubs had fun.

Did the cats cut the ham?

The cups had big red dots.

Ken got six big kit bags.

Can Kim dig up the pins?

The cap is not a hat.

Sam had ten yams to sup on.

The dog has a lot of mud on his leg.

The rat is not as big as a cat.

Mix the nuts and figs in a pan.

EXAMPLE #9 LESSON PLAN FOR LEVEL 2
All Short Vowels in CVC Words,
Introducing a Suffix: Noisy and Quiet -s

5. SPELLING WORDS

his	as	is	has	vans
lets	cups	dogs	cats	hens

6. SENTENCE DICTATION

Kim had ten cups.

The dogs had lots of pups.

His cab is red.

The pen had six hens.

Pam lets the cubs sit in the sun.

EXAMPLE #10 LESSON PLAN FOR LEVEL 2
Short Vowels with FF-LL-SS-ZZ Spelling Rule

Student/Class:	Date:	Lesson #:

NEW CONCEPT: At the end of a 1-syllable word, immediately following a single vowel, the final *f*, *l*, *s* /s/ and *z* double. When *s* is pronounced as /z/ as in his, the *s* does not double. This rule can be remembered with the phrase ***Buzz Off Miss Pill***. For further explanation on teaching spelling rules see **GWH Spelling Rule Book**.

Exceptions: *bus* (short for omnibus), *gas* (short for gasoline), *yes*, *if*, *of*, *this*, *thus*

1. ALPHABET CARD DRILL

Reading Drill

Show the student one **Alphabet Drill Card** at a time. The student writes/ traces the letter saying the letter(s) name(s), keyword and sound.
Use **Teacher Prompts** if necessary.

What is the name of this letter?
What is the keyword?
What is the sound this letter makes?

For Multiple Spellings Teacher Asks	Student Answers
What are the two sounds s makes?	*s snake /s/, s nose /z/*

a	b	c	d	e	f
g	h	i	j	k	l
m	n	o	p	r	s and s₂
t	u	v	w	x	y
z					

EXAMPLE #10 LESSON PLAN FOR LEVEL 2
Short Vowels with FF-LL-SS-ZZ
Spelling Rule

 Spelling Drill

Do not show student each **Alphabet Drill Card** and ask:

What letter spells the sounds?

The teacher says the sound and the student traces/writes the letter(s)while saying the letter name(s), keyword and sound.

For Multiple Spellings Teacher Asks	Student Answers
How many ways can you spell /k/?	c, k
How many ways can you spell /z/?	s, z

/ă/	/b/	/k/	/d/	/ĕ/	/f/
/g/	/h/	/ĭ/	/j/	/l/	/m/
/n/	/ŏ/	/p/	/r/	/s/	/t/
/ŭ/	/v/	/w/	/ks/	/y/	/z/

2. BLENDING

b		
c		ff
d		
f	a	
h		
j	e	ll
k		
l	i	
m		
p	o	ss
r		
s	u	
t		
w		zz
y		

EXAMPLE #10 LESSON PLAN FOR LEVEL 2
Short Vowels with FF-LL-SS-ZZ
Spelling Rule

3. WORD READING

bass	dill	dell	Bess	buff	cull
lass	will	fell	less	cuff	dull
mass	Bill	hell	mess	huff	gull
pass	fill	yell	Tess	muff	hull
hiss	hill	tell	ill	puff	lull
miss	mill	well	biff	ruff	mull
boss	pill	bell	tiff	off	null
loss	sill	sell	buzz	jazz	fuss
moss	till	gaff	fuzz	hiss	muss
toss	will	faff	fizz	kiss	miss

SIGHT WORDS:

a	pull	and
full	I	bull
of	the	to

4. SENTENCE READING

The den is a mess.

The doll sits on the sill.

His dog is not dull.

The bull has moss on his leg.

Pass the bell to Bess.

Tess did huff and puff on the job.

The dull boss will miss his dog.

The lass is not well.

Tell Ross not to yell.

Pull the lid off and it will fizz.

5. SPELLING WORDS

bell	will	less	hill	pass
jazz	off	well	sell	loss

6. SENTENCE DICTATION

The boss is not well, but ill.

Tess ran up the hill.

Sell the bell at a loss.

Pass the jam to Ross.

I will jazz up the dull hut.

Student/Class: **Date:**   **Lesson #:**

NEW CONCEPT: Two letters can make one sound. These are called digraphs. *ch* is taught at the beginning of words at this stage. *sh* is taught at the beginning and end of words.

1. ALPHABET CARD DRILL

Reading Drill

Show the student one **Alphabet Drill Card** at a time. The student writes/traces the letter saying the letter(s) name(s), keyword and sound.
Use **Teacher Prompts** if necessary.

What is the name of this letter?

What is the keyword?

What is the sound this letter makes?

For Multiple Spellings Teacher Asks	Student Answers
What are the two sounds s makes?	*s snake /s/, s nose /z/*

a	b	c	d	e	f
g	h	i	j	k	l
m	n	o	p	r	s and s_2
t	u	v	w	x	y
z	ch	sh			

EXAMPLE #11 LESSON PLAN FOR LEVEL 2
All Short Vowels with *ch* and *sh*
in CCVC & CVCC Words

 Spelling Drill

Do not show student each **Alphabet Drill Card** and ask:

What letter spells the sounds?

The teacher says the sound and the student traces/writes the letter(s)while saying the letter name(s), keyword and sound.

For Multiple Spellings Teacher Asks	Student Answers
How many ways can you spell /k/?	*c, k*
How many ways can you spell /z/?	*s, z*

/ă/	/b/	/k/	/d/	/ĕ/	/f/
/g/	/h/	/ĭ/	/j/	/l/	/m/
/n/	/ŏ/	/p/	/r/	/s/	/t/
/ŭ/	/v/	/w/	/ks/	/y/	/z/
/ch/	/sh/				

2. BLENDING

b		
c	a	g
ch		
d	e	n
f		
l	i	p
m		
r	o	sh
s		
sh	u	t
w		

GREAT WORD HOUSE
Reading & Spelling Program

3. WORD READING

chip	chin	shin	chap	shop	chat
chad	shot	sham	Shep	shim	Chet
bash	mesh	fish	shut	chop	chum
rash	rush	chug	cash	ship	posh
sash	wish	shun	sham	chit	dish
mash	gash	Josh	gush	mush	lush

SIGHT WORDS:

a	pull	and
full	I	push
of	the	to

4. SENTENCE READING

Josh can chat at the shop.

Chop the logs at the dam.

Josh can dish up the mash.

Dan had bad fish and has a rash.

The till in the shop is full of cash.

I wish I had a posh van.

The chap shot at the rat.

The dog will rush at the cat.

Shep has mud on his chin.

Chet will pull and push his dog to the vet.

EXAMPLE #11 LESSON PLAN FOR LEVEL 2
All Short Vowels with *ch* and *sh*
in CCVC & CVCC Words

5. SPELLING WORDS

shop	shut	chap	chin	fish
ship	chum	mash	wish	rush

6. SENTENCE DICTATION

The ship has a lot of fish.

The chap had a wish.

Shep has cash to shop.

Mash up the cod, Chet.

Shut the shop and rush to the hut.

EXAMPLE #12 LESSON PLAN FOR LEVEL 2
All Short Vowels with *th* and *th₂* in CCVC & CVCC Words

Student/Class: **Date:**   **Lesson #:**

NEW CONCEPT: Two letters that make one sound is called a digraph.
th is a digraph and has two phoneme pronunciations. *th* can be a quiet sound /th/ as in thumb or noisy as in there. Noisy *th* is the second sound of th (*th₂* or *th*). Quiet letters are also called 'unvoiced' and noisy letters are called 'voiced'.

1. ALPHABET CARD DRILL

Reading Drill

Show the student one **Alphabet Drill Card** at a time. The student writes/traces the letter saying the letter(s) name(s), keyword and sound.
Use **Teacher Prompts** if necessary.

What is the name of this letter?

What is the keyword?

What is the sound this letter makes?

For Multiple Spellings Teacher Asks	Student Answers
What are the two sounds s makes?	*s snake /s/, s nose /z/*
What are the two sounds th makes?	*th thumb /th/, th there /th/*

a	b	c	d	e	f
g	h	i	j	k	l
m	n	o	p	r	s and s₂
t	u	v	w	x	y
z	ch	sh	th and th₂		

EXAMPLE #12 LESSON PLAN FOR LEVEL 2
All Short Vowels with *th* and *th₂*
in CCVC & CVCC Words

 Spelling Drill

Do not show student each **Alphabet Drill Card** and ask:

What letter spells the sounds?

The teacher says the sound and the student traces/writes the letter(s) while saying the letter name(s), keyword and sound.

For Multiple Spellings Teacher Asks	Student Answers
How many ways can you spell /k/?	c, k
How many ways can you spell /z/?	s, z

/ă/	/b/	/k/	/d/	/ĕ/	/f/
/g/	/h/	/ĭ/	/j/	/l/	/m/
/n/	/ŏ/	/p/	/r/	/s/	/t/
/ŭ/	/v/	/w/	/ks/	/y/	/z/
/ch/	/sh/	/th/	/th/		

2. BLENDING

b		d
	a	
h		g
	e	
m		m
	i	
p		n
	o	
th		s
	u	
th₂		t
w		th

Page 56

greatwordhouse.com All rights reserved © 2018.

EXAMPLE #12 LESSON PLAN FOR LEVEL 2
All Short Vowels with *th* and *th₂*
in CCVC & CVCC Words

3. WORD READING

bath	path	pith	Beth	thin	than	this
math	moth	with	Seth	thug	that	thus
hath	Goth	kith	doth	thud	then	them

SIGHT WORDS:

a	and	I
of	the	to

4. SENTENCE READING

Seth got a moth in his cup.

This is a big red van.

That is the path to the hut.

Cut the logs and lug them to the dam.

I had a dip and then sat in the sun.

A moth had a bit of pith.

The bath is hot, and I will not get in.

The thin lad had a dish of cod.

This math sum is not fun.

His kith and kin had a lot of cash.

5. SPELLING WORDS

this	that	them	then	math
bath	path	with	moth	thud

6. SENTENCE DICTATION

That map has a path.

I got in the van with them.

The moth is in the bath.

I can fix that math sum.

I had a bath, and then I had a nap.

EXAMPLE #13 LESSON PLAN FOR LEVEL 2
All Short Vowels with *-ck*
in CVCC & CCVCC Words

GREAT WORD HOUSE
Reading & Spelling Program

SCOPE & SEQUENCE
S
LEVELS 1-4

Student/Class: Date: Lesson #:

NEW CONCEPT: Two letters that make one sound is called a digraph.
-ck is a digraph and is found at the end of a 1-syllable word, immediately after the vowel.

1. ALPHABET CARD DRILL

 Reading Drill
Show the student one **Alphabet Drill Card** at a time. The student writes/traces the letter saying the letter(s) name(s), keyword and sound.
Use **Teacher Prompts** if necessary.
What is the name of this letter?
What is the keyword?
What is the sound this letter makes?

For Multiple Spellings Teacher Asks	Student Answers
What are the two sounds s makes?	*s snake /s/, s nose /z/*
What are the two sounds th makes?	*th thumb /th/, th there /th/*

a	b	c	d	e	f
g	h	i	j	k	l
m	n	o	p	r	s and s$_2$
t	u	v	w	x	y
z	ch	ck	sh	th and th$_2$	

 Spelling Drill

Do not show student each **Alphabet Drill Card** and ask:

What letter spells the sounds?

The teacher says the sound and the student traces/writes the letter(s)while saying the letter name(s), keyword and sound.

For Multiple Spellings Teacher Asks	Student Answers
How many ways can you spell /k/?	c, k, ck
How many ways can you spell /z/?	s, z

/ă/	/b/	/k/	/d/	/ĕ/	/f/
/g/	/h/	/ĭ/	/j/	/l/	/m/
/n/	/ŏ/	/p/	/r/	/s/	/t/
/ŭ/	/v/	/w/	/ks/	/y/	/z/
/ch/	/sh/	/th/	/<u>th</u>/		

EXAMPLE #13 LESSON PLAN FOR LEVEL 2
All Short Vowels with *-ck*
in CVCC & CCVCC Words

2. BLENDING

b d h j l m n p r s t w y ch sh th	a e i o u	ck

3. WORD READING

back	buck	rack	rock	sack	sock
neck	tock	tack	tuck	sick	suck
dock	duck	deck	heck	hack	Nick
muck	Mick	lack	lick	luck	pick
pack	puck	tack	tick	wack	wick
thick	shack	shock	check	Chuck	chick

EXAMPLE #13 LESSON PLAN FOR LEVEL 2
All Short Vowels with *-ck*
in CVCC & CCVCC Words

SIGHT WORDS:

a	and	I
of	the	to
was		

4. SENTENCE READING

The back of the deck is a mess.

Pick up that bat and pass it to Chuck.

The shack is at the top of the hill.

The thick sock is in the shed.

Mick had a lot of luck.

The duck is in the sack.

Nick has a sick dog.

The puck is in the net.

The chick had a peck at the sack of cobs.

Dan had a lot of muck on his neck.

5. SPELLING WORDS

duck	sick	deck	luck	sack
sock	lock	neck	thick	check

6. SENTENCE DICTATION

That duck has a bad leg.

Tell them to lug the sack to the deck.

Shut the shed and lock it up.

His neck got red in the sun.

Mick was sick, and I had to check on him.

EXAMPLE #14 LESSON PLAN FOR LEVEL 2
All Short Vowels with *qu* in CCVC & CCVCC Words

Student/Class: Date: Lesson #:

NEW CONCEPT: *q* makes the sound /k/, but it is always followed by *u* which is pronounced /w/. *qu* is taught as a common consonant cluster which is pronounced /kw/. In a few words, the *u* is silent.

1. ALPHABET CARD DRILL

Reading Drill
Show the student one **Alphabet Drill Card** at a time. The student writes/traces the letter saying the letter(s) name(s), keyword and sound.
Use **Teacher Prompts** if necessary.

What is the name of this letter?
What is the keyword?
What is the sound this letter makes?

For Multiple Spellings Teacher Asks	Student Answers
What are the two sounds s makes?	*s snake /s/, s nose /z/*
What are the two sounds th makes?	*th thumb /th/, th there /th/*

a	b	c	d	e	f
g	h	i	j	k	l
m	n	o	p	qu	r
s and s₂	t	u	v	w	x
y	z	ch	ck	sh	th and th₂

EXAMPLE #14 LESSON PLAN FOR LEVEL 2
All Short Vowels with *qu*
in CCVC & CCVCC Words

 Spelling Drill

Do not show student each **Alphabet Drill Card** and ask:

What letter spells the sounds?

The teacher says the sound and the student traces/writes the letter(s)while saying the letter name(s), keyword and sound.

For Multiple Spellings Teacher Asks	Student Answers
How many ways can you spell /k/?	c, k, ck
How many ways can you spell /z/?	s, z

/ă/	/b/	/k/	/d/	/ĕ/	/f/
/g/	/h/	/ĭ/	/j/	/l/	/m/
/n/	/ŏ/	/p/	/kw/	/r/	/s/
/t/	/ŭ/	/v/	/w/	/ks/	/y/
/z/	/ch/	/sh/	/th/	/<u>th</u>/	

2. BLENDING

		d
	a	ll
	e	n
qu	i	t
	o	z
	u	
		ck

EXAMPLE #14 LESSON PLAN FOR LEVEL 2
All Short Vowels with *qu*
in CCVC & CCVCC Words

3. WORD READING

quack	quit	quill	quid	quoth
quick	quiz	quip	quell	quin

SIGHT WORDS:

a	and	I
of	the	to
was		

4. SENTENCE READING

That math quiz is not fun.

If the dog is quick, it will nab the ham.

Mick will not quit this job.

"A dog is not cat," quoth the man.

I will bet six quid that dog will win.

I can not jot with a quill.

Beth can quip with Seth.

That duck did not quack.

EXAMPLE #14 LESSON PLAN FOR LEVEL 2
All Short Vowels with *qu*
in CCVC & CCVCC Words

5. SPELLING WORDS

quin	quick	quack	quell	quiz
quit	quip	quill	quoth	quid

6. SENTENCE DICTATION

I had six quid in the till.

A duck can quack.

The quip was not bad.

A math quiz is fun.

This dog is quick, but that cat is not.

EXAMPLE #15 LESSON PLAN FOR LEVEL 2
Cumulative Review for Short Vowels:
CVC, CCVC, CVCC, CCVCC and Suffix –s

Student/Class: **Date:**   **Lesson #:**

REVIEW CONCEPT: A suffix is added to the end of a word. The suffix –s comes at the end of the word. The hyphen indicates the point of attachment to the word. Suffix -s has two jobs:

1. *–s* makes nouns plural, e.g. dogs, cats.
2. *–s* is used with 3rd person singular verbs in the present tense or he/she/it verbs: *He nods. She sits. It naps.* You can use a proper or common noun instead of he/she/it: *Tom nods. Pam sits. A cat naps.*

1. ALPHABET CARD DRILL

Reading Drill

Show the student one **Alphabet Drill Card** at a time. The student writes/ traces the letter saying the letter(s) name(s), keyword and sound.

Use **Teacher Prompts** if necessary.

What is the name of this letter?

What is the keyword?

What is the sound this letter makes?

For Multiple Spellings Teacher Asks	Student Answers
What are the two sounds s makes?	*s snake /s/, s nose /z/*
What are the two sounds th makes?	*th thumb /th/, th there /th/*

a	b	c	d	e	f
g	h	i	j	k	l
m	n	o	p	qu	r
s and s₂	t	u	v	w	x
y	z	ch	ck	sh	th and th₂

 Spelling Drill

Do not show student each **Alphabet Drill Card** and ask:

What letter spells the sounds?

The teacher says the sound and the student traces/writes the letter(s)while saying the letter name(s), keyword and sound.

For Multiple Spellings Teacher Asks	Student Answers
How many ways can you spell /k/?	*c, k, ck*
How many ways can you spell /z/?	*s, z*

/ă/	/b/	/k/	/d/	/ĕ/	/f/
/g/	/h/	/ĭ/	/j/	/l/	/m/
/n/	/ŏ/	/p/	/kw/	/r/	/s/
/t/	/ŭ/	/v/	/w/	/ks/	/y/
/z/	/ch/	/sh/	/th/	/th/	

Suffix Drill

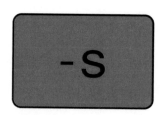

After the **Alphabet Card Drill**, tell the student that suffixes come at the end and are on red cards (red for 'stop'). The hyphen shows where the suffix is fixed or joined to the word.

Teacher: *Please read the card.*
Student: *–s says /s/ and /z/*
Teacher: *What are the jobs of suffix –s?*
Student: *It shows plural (more than one), e.g. cats. It is used with he/she/it verbs, e.g. He digs. She sits. It yaps. Proper and common nouns can be used instead of he/she/it.*

EXAMPLE #15 LESSON PLAN FOR LEVEL 2
Cumulative Review for Short Vowels:
CVC, CCVC, CVCC, CCVCC and Suffix *–s*

2. BLENDING

Add *–s* to all the words below. Look at the last letter in the word. If it is noisy then the *–s* will be noisy. Underline *–s/z/*. If the last letter in the word is quiet, the *–s* will be quiet. Circle *–s/s/*.

CVC	CCVC	CVCC	CCVCC
cat__	chat__	fill__	shack__
dog__	chip__	sock__	quill__
leg__	shop__	huff__	check__
cup__	thug__	sell__	shell__
mug__	shun__	math__	chaff__
pin__	thud__	lock__	quell__
win__	chum__	cuff__	chick__
bit__	shed__	bath__	chill__
sit__	chop__	tiff__	chuck__
rub__	ship__	tick__	chuff__
hum__	quit__	pill__	shock__
bat__	shut__	moth__	shuck__

EXAMPLE #15 LESSON PLAN FOR LEVEL 2
Cumulative Review for Short Vowels:
CVC, CCVC, CVCC, CCVCC and Suffix –s

3. WORD READING

CVC	CCVC	CVCC	CCVCC
cats	chats	fills	shacks
dogs	chips	socks	quills
legs	shops	huffs	checks
cups	thugs	sells	shells
mugs	shuns	maths	chaffs
pins	thuds	locks	quells
wins	chums	cuffs	chicks
bits	sheds	baths	chills
sits	chops	tiffs	chucks
rubs	ships	ticks	chuffs
hums	quits	pills	shocks
bats	shuts	moths	shucks

SIGHT WORDS:

a	and	I
of	the	to

EXAMPLE #15 LESSON PLAN FOR LEVEL 2
Cumulative Review for Short Vowels: CVC, CCVC, CVCC, CCVCC and Suffix –s

4. SENTENCE READING

The ships can dock at six.

Did the cats nab the chicks?

The lad chats with his pal.

The dog rubs the red dot on his leg.

Can Chet get the mud off his socks?

The moths got a zap in the shack.

The rat shocks the fox.

Beth checks the locks on the shacks.

The mad mob yells, and Shep quells them.

Sam shucks the shells off.

5. SPELLING WORDS

bats	dogs	huffs	tells	pills
lets	licks	shuts	quits	checks

6. SENTENCE DICTATION

Shep has ten bats.

The dogs had lots of pups.

A lad huffs up the hill.

The boss quits the job.

Seth checks on the pigs in the pen.

EXAMPLE #16 LESSON PLAN FOR LEVEL 2
All Short Vowels in CVC, CVCC Words
with Suffix –es

Student/Class: **Date:**   **Lesson #:**

NEW CONCEPT: The schwa is a lazy vowel sound. Any vowel can turn into a schwa. It occurs in unstressed syllables and in a few one-syllable words, e.g. *the* and *a*. It is represented by the symbol ə. It sounds like "uh". For example, *a* in **med**al, *e* **jack**et, *i* in **hab**it, *o* in **mel**on, and second *u* in **ruck**us. The stressed syllable is in bold.

NEW CONCEPT: The suffix –*es* is an unstressed syllable and the vowel *e* is a schwa. –*es* is pronounced /əz/. –*es* is used instead of –*s* and does the same jobs. We use –*es* instead of –*s* because we need to hear the suffix and the vowel sound helps us to hear it. After some letters or digraphs it is hard to hear and pronounce the /s/ or /z/ sound. Ask the student to try and say a list of words adding the suffix –*s* to: *bus, wish, fuss, buzz, fix*.

Suffix -es has two jobs:

1. –*es* makes nouns plural, e.g. dishes, passes.
2. –*es* is used with 3rd person singular verbs in the present tense or he/she/it verbs: He wishes. She fixes. It kisses. You can use a proper or common noun instead of he/she/it: Tom rush*es*. Pam wish*es*. A dog kiss*es*.

   *Note: many words are nouns and verbs, e.g. *fix, wish, rush, kiss*

EXAMPLE #16 LESSON PLAN FOR LEVEL 2
All Short Vowels in CVC, CVCC Words
with Suffix –es

1. ALPHABET CARD DRILL

 Reading Drill

Show the student one **Alphabet Drill Card** at a time. The student writes/ traces the letter saying the letter(s) name(s), keyword and sound.

Use **Teacher Prompts** if necessary.

What is the name of this letter?

What is the keyword?

What is the sound this letter makes?

For Multiple Spellings Teacher Asks	Student Answers
What are the two sounds s makes?	*s snake /s/, s nose /z/*
What are the two sounds th makes?	*th thumb /th/, th there /th/*

a	b	c	d	e	f
g	h	i	j	k	l
m	n	o	p	qu	r
s and s₂	t	u	v	w	x
y	z	ch	ck	sh	th and th₂

EXAMPLE #16 LESSON PLAN FOR LEVEL 2
All Short Vowels in CVC, CVCC Words
with Suffix –es

 Spelling Drill

Do not show student each **Alphabet Drill Card** and ask:

What letter spells the sounds?

The teacher says the sound and the student traces/writes the letter(s)while saying the letter name(s), keyword and sound.

For Multiple Spellings Teacher Asks	Student Answers
How many ways can you spell /k/?	c, k, ck
How many ways can you spell /z/?	s, z

/ă/	/b/	/k/	/d/	/ě/	/f/
/g/	/h/	/ĭ/	/j/	/l/	/m/
/n/	/ŏ/	/p/	/kw/	/r/	/s/
/t/	/ŭ/	/v/	/w/	/ks/	/y/
/z/	/ch/	/sh/	/th/	/<u>th</u>/	

Suffix Drill

-es

After the **Alphabet Card Drill**, tell the student that suffixes come at the end and are on red cards (red for 'stop'). The hyphen shows where the suffix is fixed or joined to the word.

Teacher: *Please read the card.*
Student: *-es says /əz/.*
Teacher: *What are the jobs of suffix –es?*
Student: *It shows plural (more than one), e.g. kisses. It is used with he/she/it verbs, e.g. He fishes. She rushes. It messes. Proper and common nouns can be used instead of he/she/it.*

*Note that some words are nouns and verbs, e.g. wishes, kisses

EXAMPLE #16 LESSON PLAN FOR LEVEL 2
All Short Vowels in CVC, CVCC Words with Suffix –es

GREAT WORD HOUSE
Reading & Spelling Program

SCOPE & SEQUENCE 4-1 LEVELS **S**

2. BLENDING

Look at the last letter or digraph in the word. If is makes the sound /s/, /sh/ or /ks/ add –es.

cat	
dog	
moth	
*push	-s
mass	
math	
wish	
fix	-es
path	
rush	
tell	
mix	
fuss	

* Sight word optional

3. WORD READING

foxes	masses	wishes	gashes	dashes
boxes	lasses	mashes	cashes	bashes
taxes	losses	lashes	dishes	passes
fixes	bosses	fishes	hushes	tosses
vexes	fusses	rushes	noshes	messes

EXAMPLE #16 LESSON PLAN FOR LEVEL 2
All Short Vowels in CVC, CVCC Words
with Suffix –es

SIGHT WORDS:

a	and	I
of	the	to
are	was	pushes
bushes		

4. SENTENCE READING

The taxes on the set of dishes are a lot.

Did the foxes nab the hen?

Masses of moss are in the bushes.

The cups are in the boxes.

The boss was mad at the big losses.

A dog pushes his dish.

Jim wishes his dog had a bath.

Ben hushes the tot.

Dad fixes the mess in his cab.

Pam fishes and tosses the fish back.

5. SPELLING WORDS

fixes	passes	wishes	messes	tosses
boxes	fusses	bashes	fishes	rushes

EXAMPLE #16 LESSON PLAN FOR LEVEL 2
All Short Vowels in CVC, CVCC Words
with Suffix *-es*

6. SENTENCE DICTATION

Kim can fill up the boxes.

Dan passes Sam on his run.

Mom had six wishes.

Ben rushes to his job.

Seth messes the den and then fixes it.

EXAMPLE #17 LESSON PLAN FOR LEVEL 2
Cumulative Review Short Vowels with Suffixes –es and –s

Student/Class: Date: Lesson #:

REVIEW CONCEPT: A suffix is added to the end of a word. The suffixes –s and –es have two jobs:

1. makes nouns plural, e.g. dog*s*, cat*s*, wish*es*, kiss*es*
2. used with 3rd person singular verbs in the present tense or he/she/it verbs:

     He nod*s*. She sit*s*. It nap*s*.

     He fish*es*. She wish*es*. It mess*es*.

1. ALPHABET CARD DRILL

Reading Drill

Show the student one **Alphabet Drill Card** at a time. The student writes/traces the letter saying the letter(s) name(s), keyword and sound.

Use **Teacher Prompts** if necessary.

What is the name of this letter?

What is the keyword?

What is the sound this letter makes?

For Multiple Spellings Teacher Asks	Student Answers
What are the two sounds s makes?	*s snake /s/, s nose /z/*
What are the two sounds th makes?	*th thumb /th/, th there /th/*

a	b	c	d	e	f
g	h	i	j	k	l
m	n	o	p	qu	r
s and s$_2$	t	u	v	w	x
y	z	ch	ck	sh	th and th$_2$

EXAMPLE #17 LESSON PLAN FOR LEVEL 2
Cumulative Review Short Vowels with Suffixes –*es* and –*s*

 Spelling Drill

Do not show student each **Alphabet Drill Card** and ask:

What letter spells the sounds?

The teacher says the sound and the student traces/writes the letter(s)while saying the letter name(s), keyword and sound.

For Multiple Spellings Teacher Asks	Student Answers
How many ways can you spell /k/?	*c, k, ck*
How many ways can you spell /z/?	*s, z*

/ă/	/b/	/k/	/d/	/ě/	/f/
/g/	/h/	/ĭ/	/j/	/l/	/m/
/n/	/ŏ/	/p/	/kw/	/r/	/s/
/t/	/ŭ/	/v/	/w/	/ks/	/y/
/z/	/ch/	/sh/	/th/	/<u>th</u>/	

Suffix Drill

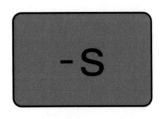

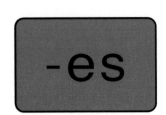

Teacher: *Please read the cards.*

Student: *–s says /s/ and /z/; -es says /əz/.*

Teacher: *What are the jobs of suffix –s and –es?*

Student: *They show plural (more than one), e.g. cats, kisses. They are used with he/she/it verbs, e.g. He digs. She sits. It yaps. He fishes. She rushes. It messes. Proper and common nouns can be used instead of he/she/it.*

2. BLENDING

Add –s or –es to all the words below.

CVC	CCVC	CVCC	CCVCC
cat___	chat___	fill___	shack___
fox___	chip___	sock___	quill___
leg___	shop___	mass___	check___
cup___	thug___	sell___	shell___
tax___	shun___	dish___	shush___
pin___	quiz___	loss___	chick___
box___	chum___	cuff___	chill___
pod___	shed___	bash___	chuck___
six___	chop___	miss___	shock___
rub___	ship___	tick___	chuff___
hum___	quit___	pill___	shock___
fax___	shut___	buzz___	shuck___

3. WORD READING

CVC	CCVC	CVCC	CCVCC
cats	chats	fills	shacks
foxes	chips	socks	quills
legs	shops	masses	checks
cups	thugs	sells	shells
taxes	shuns	dishes	shushes
pins	*quizzes	losses	chicks
boxes	chums	cuffs	chills
pods	sheds	bashes	chucks
sixes	chops	misses	shocks
rubs	ships	ticks	chuffs
hums	quits	pills	shocks
faxes	shuts	buzzes	shucks

*need to know 111 Doubling Rule

EXAMPLE #17 LESSON PLAN FOR LEVEL 2
Cumulative Review Short Vowels with Suffixes –es and –s

SIGHT WORDS:

a	and	I
of	the	to
are	was	pushes
bushes		

4. SENTENCE READING

The tug pushes the ship to the dock.

The chicks are in the bushes.

The foxes can nab the hens.

Len checks the chips on the dishes.

A cat hisses at the rats in the den.

The boss sobs at the cash losses.

Dad had boxes of bats and caps.

Sid misses the bus and jogs to his job.

Pam runs laps and passes six pals.

The hog noshes on masses of pods.

5. SPELLING WORDS

bats	losses	rushes	wishes	shushes
checks	foxes	sixes	pens	baths

6. SENTENCE DICTATION

Shep wishes he had lots of pens.

Mom shushes the dog as it sets up a din.

A lad rushes up the hill and huffs and puffs.

Lots of losses led the bosses to quit.

Seth checks on the hens as the foxes nab them.

Mom rushes the kids to the bath.

The bug buzzes and the cat hisses.

Kim fixes the mess and then chops the logs.

GREAT WORD HOUSE
Reading & Spelling Program

EXAMPLE #18 LESSON PLAN FOR LEVEL 3
All Short Vowels, Initial Consonant Clusters
fl-, sl-, sm-, sn-

Student/Class: **Date:** **Lesson #:**

NEW CONCEPT: A consonant cluster refers to consonants that commonly occur together. These clusters are taught first as they are easy to blend together and pronounce.

1. ALPHABET CARD DRILL

Reading Drill
Show the student one **Alphabet Drill Card** at a time. The student writes/traces the letter saying the letter(s) name(s), keyword and sound.
Use **Teacher Prompts** if necessary.
What is the name of this letter?
What is the keyword?
What is the sound this letter makes?

For Multiple Spellings Teacher Asks	Student Answers
What are the two sounds s makes?	*s snake /s/, s nose /z/*
What are the two sounds th makes?	*th thumb /th/, th there /th/*

a	b	c	d	e	f
g	h	i	j	k	l
m	n	o	p	qu	r
s and s_2	t	u	v	w	x
y	z	ch	ck	sh	th and th_2

 Spelling Drill

Do not show student each **Alphabet Drill Card** and ask:

What letter spells the sounds?

The teacher says the sound and the student traces/writes the letter(s)while saying the letter name(s), keyword and sound.

For Multiple Spellings Teacher Asks	Student Answers
How many ways can you spell /k/?	*c, k, ck*
How many ways can you spell /z/?	*s, z*

/ă/	/b/	/k/	/d/	/ĕ/	/f/
/g/	/h/	/ĭ/	/j/	/l/	/m/
/n/	/ŏ/	/p/	/kw/	/r/	/s/
/t/	/ŭ/	/v/	/w/	/ks/	/y/
/z/	/ch/	/sh/	/th/	/t͟h/	

2. BLENDING

		b
		d
fl		g
sl	a	m
fr	e	n
	i	
sm	o	p
sn	u	t
qu		x
		z

EXAMPLE #18 LESSON PLAN FOR LEVEL 3
All Short Vowels, Initial Consonant Clusters
fl-, sl-, sm-, sn-

3. WORD READING

flat	flip	slid	snag	slat	slim
flab	flit	slab	snap	sled	slip
flop	flan	slob	snub	slog	slop
flag	flog	slug	snug	slum	smug
flap	fled	slit	snit	slap	quit

SIGHT WORDS:

a	and	I
of	the	to
was		

4. SENTENCE READING

The dog fled as the cat ran at him.

Tim set the flag on top of the hut.

The man quit his job in a snit.

Sam slid on the sled.

A slim lad had a bit of flan.

The snug slug had a nap.

Pam will slip in the wet mud.

The bug sat on a slat.

His rod can snap if the cod is big.

Set the slab on the flat sod.

EXAMPLE #18 LESSON PLAN FOR LEVEL 3
All Short Vowels, Initial Consonant Clusters
fl-, sl-, sm-, sn-

5. SPELLING WORDS

flat	slip	flag	smug	quiz
snug	slog	flip	fled	quit

6. SENTENCE DICTATION

I quit the job as it was bad.

A flag can flap a lot.

Tim got mad at his dog and he fled.

It is a slog to run ten laps.

The cat had a nap in the snug box.

EXAMPLE #19 LESSON PLAN FOR LEVEL 3
All Short Vowels, Initial Consonant Clusters
bl-, cl-, fl-, gl-, pl-, sl-
in CCVC Words

Student/Class: Date: Lesson #:

NEW CONCEPT: A consonant cluster refers to consonants that commonly occur together. These clusters are all *l* clusters.

1. ALPHABET CARD DRILL

   Reading Drill

Show the student one **Alphabet Drill Card** at a time. The student writes/traces the letter saying the letter(s) name(s), keyword and sound.

Use **Teacher Prompts** if necessary.

What is the name of this letter?

What is the keyword?

What is the sound this letter makes?

For Multiple Spellings Teacher Asks	Student Answers
What are the two sounds s makes?	*s snake /s/, s nose /z/*
What are the two sounds th makes?	*th thumb /th/, th there /th/*

a	b	c	d	e	f
g	h	i	j	k	l
m	n	o	p	qu	r
s and s₂	t	u	v	w	x
y	z	ch	ck	sh	th and th₂

EXAMPLE #19 LESSON PLAN FOR LEVEL 3
All Short Vowels, Initial Consonant Clusters
bl-, cl-, fl-, gl-, pl-, sl-
in CCVC Words

 Spelling Drill

Do not show student each **Alphabet Drill Card** and ask:

What letter spells the sounds?

The teacher says the sound and the student traces/writes the letter(s)while saying the letter name(s), keyword and sound.

For Multiple Spellings Teacher Asks	Student Answers
How many ways can you spell /k/?	c, k, ck
How many ways can you spell /z/?	s, z

/ă/	/b/	/k/	/d/	/ĕ/	/f/
/g/	/h/	/ĭ/	/j/	/l/	/m/
/n/	/ŏ/	/p/	/kw/	/r/	/s/
/t/	/ŭ/	/v/	/w/	/ks/	/y/
/z/	/ch/	/sh/	/th/	/th/	

2. BLENDING

bl		b
cl	a	d
fl	e	g
gl	i	m
pl	o	n
sl	u	p
		t
		x
		z

3. WORD READING

clap	glad	flax	plop	slum
clop	glen	flub	plan	slap
clad	glum	flip	pled	slog
clip	glug	flex	plod	slit
flat	glut	slid	slim	sled
flab	flit	slab	slip	fled
flop	flan	slob	slop	flap
flag	flog	slug	slat	clan

SIGHT WORDS:

a	and	I
of	the	to
was		

4. SENTENCE READING

The clan fled to the glen.

Ben had a plan to set up the flag.

The man quit the job as it was a slog.

Slim Sam slid on the sled.

A glad dog fed on a bit of flan.

The slug had a nap on a flat slab.

Pam will slip in the wet slop.

The pig fed on a bag of flax.

His flag can flap on top of the hut.

I did not clap at the bad plan.

GREAT
WORD
HOUSE
Reading & Spelling
Program

EXAMPLE #19 LESSON PLAN FOR LEVEL 3
All Short Vowels, Initial Consonant Clusters
bl-, cl-, fl-, gl-, pl-, sl-
in CCVC Words

5. SPELLING WORDS

flat	slip	flag	plan	slog
clap	clan	flip	fled	glad

6. SENTENCE DICTATION

I was glad to get rid of the wet slug.

Val did a flip and slid on his tum.

The cat fled and the dog did yap.

It is a slog to run laps at the dam.

The glum rat had a bit of flan.

EXAMPLE #20 LESSON PLAN FOR LEVEL 3
All Short Vowels, Initial Consonant Clusters
br-, cr-, dr-, fr-, gr-, pr-, tr-
in CCVC Words

GREAT WORD HOUSE ™
Reading & Spelling Program

SCOPE & SEQUENCE **S** *LEVELS 1-4*

Student/Class: Date: Lesson #:

NEW CONCEPT: A consonant cluster refers to consonants that commonly occur together. These clusters are all *r* clusters.

1. ALPHABET CARD DRILL

Reading Drill

Show the student one **Alphabet Drill Card** at a time. The student writes/traces the letter saying the letter(s) name(s), keyword and sound.

Use **Teacher Prompts** if necessary.

What is the name of this letter?

What is the keyword?

What is the sound this letter makes?

For Multiple Spellings Teacher Asks	Student Answers
What are the two sounds s makes?	*s snake /s/, s nose /z/*
What are the two sounds th makes?	*th thumb /th/, th there /th/*

a	b	c	d	e	f
g	h	i	j	k	l
m	n	o	p	qu	r
s and s$_2$	t	u	v	w	x
y	z	ch	ck	sh	th and th$_2$

EXAMPLE #20 LESSON PLAN FOR LEVEL 3
All Short Vowels, Initial Consonant Clusters
br-, cr-, dr-, fr-, gr-, pr-, tr-
in CCVC Words

 Spelling Drill

Do not show student each **Alphabet Drill Card** and ask:

What letter spells the sounds?

The teacher says the sound and the student traces/writes the letter(s)while saying the letter name(s), keyword and sound.

For Multiple Spellings Teacher Asks	Student Answers
How many ways can you spell /k/?	*c, k, ck*
How many ways can you spell /z/?	*s, z*

/ă/	/b/	/k/	/d/	/ĕ/	/f/
/g/	/h/	/ĭ/	/j/	/l/	/m/
/n/	/ŏ/	/p/	/kw/	/r/	/s/
/t/	/ŭ/	/v/	/w/	/ks/	/y/
/z/	/ch/	/sh/	/th/	/<u>th</u>/	

2. BLENDING

br		
	a	b
cr		d
	e	g
fr		m
	i	n
gr		p
	o	t
pr		x
	u	
tr		

EXAMPLE #20 LESSON PLAN FOR LEVEL 3
All Short Vowels, Initial Consonant Clusters
br-, cr-, dr-, fr-, gr-, pr-, tr-
in CCVC Words

GREAT WORD HOUSE
Reading & Spelling Program

SCOPE & SEQUENCE
S
LEVELS 4-1

3. WORD READING

brag	crop	drip	frog	grad	prod
crab	trim	from	grim	prom	drop
drag	Fred	grin	pram	tram	brim
trod	prep	grab	Fran	dram	crud
fret	drat	crag	brat	trap	grid
gram	trot	cram	Brit	drum	crux
Greg	Brad	trip	prim	prig	drub
Trev	Bret	crib	brig	prop	bran

SIGHT WORDS:

a	and	I
of	the	to
was	into	

GREAT WORD HOUSE
Reading & Spelling
Program

EXAMPLE #20 LESSON PLAN FOR LEVEL 3
All Short Vowels, Initial Consonant Clusters
br-, cr-, dr-, fr-, gr-, pr-, tr-
in CCVC Words

SCOPE & SEQUENCE
S
LEVELS 1-4

4. SENTENCE READING

Trev and Brad can drum at the prom.

A gram of bran is not a lot.

The crab ran from the trap.

Gran has a frog as a pet.

I had to cram into the tram.

A drop of mud did drip on the mat.

Brad had a big grin at grad.

Bret and Fran brag a lot.

If I prod the frog, it can hop.

It was a drag at the hut, and Fred was grim.

5. SPELLING WORDS

cram	gram	brim	trim	drag
frog	trap	drum	drop	from

GREAT WORD HOUSE
Reading & Spelling Program

EXAMPLE #20 LESSON PLAN FOR LEVEL 3
All Short Vowels, Initial Consonant Clusters
br-, cr-, dr-, fr-, gr-, pr-, tr-
in CCVC Words

6. SENTENCE DICTATION

Trev had to trim his dog.

The frog can hop from the tub to the mat.

A drop of gum can drip from the brim.

Drag the drum to the prom.

A gram of fat is not a lot.

EXAMPLE #21 LESSON PLAN FOR LEVEL 3
All Short Vowels, Initial Consonant Clusters
sc-, sk-, sm-, sn-, sp-, st-, sw-
in CCVC Words

GREAT WORD HOUSE Reading & Spelling Program

Student/Class:	Date:	Lesson #:

NEW CONCEPT: A consonant cluster refers to consonants that commonly occur together. *S* is quiet at the beginning of words, so these clusters all begin with quiet /s/.

1. ALPHABET CARD DRILL

Reading Drill

Show the student one **Alphabet Drill Card** at a time. The student writes/traces the letter saying the letter(s) name(s), keyword and sound.

Use **Teacher Prompts** if necessary.

What is the name of this letter?

What is the keyword?

What is the sound this letter makes?

For Multiple Spellings Teacher Asks	Student Answers
What are the two sounds s makes?	*s snake /s/, s nose /z/*
What are the two sounds th makes?	*th thumb /th/, th there /th/*

a	b	c	d	e	f
g	h	i	j	k	l
m	n	o	p	qu	r
s and s₂	t	u	v	w	x
y	z	ch	ck	sh	th and th₂

GREAT WORD HOUSE
Reading & Spelling Program

EXAMPLE #21 LESSON PLAN FOR LEVEL 3
All Short Vowels, Initial Consonant Clusters
sc-, sk-, sm-, sn-, sp-, st-, sw-
in CCVC Words

 Spelling Drill

Do not show student each **Alphabet Drill Card** and ask:

What letter spells the sounds?

The teacher says the sound and the student traces/writes the letter(s)while saying the letter name(s), keyword and sound.

For Multiple Spellings Teacher Asks	Student Answers
How many ways can you spell /k/?	*c, k, ck*
How many ways can you spell /z/?	*s, z*

/ă/	/b/	/k/	/d/	/ĕ/	/f/
/g/	/h/	/ĭ/	/j/	/l/	/m/
/n/	/ŏ/	/p/	/kw/	/r/	/s/
/t/	/ŭ/	/v/	/w/	/ks/	/y/
/z/	/ch/	/sh/	/th/	/<u>th</u>/	

2. BLENDING

Add an *s* and read the word

__cat	__mug	__nug	__pit	__cum	__kit
__nap	__pat	__mog	__wig	__kid	__lot
__lat	__lim	__lam	__led	__kim	__tag
__tep	__lip	__nub	__tun	__wag	__wot
__lap	__wop	__nob	__nag	__tab	__lab
__can	__lop	__wim	__wam	__kin	_tem

EXAMPLE #21 LESSON PLAN FOR LEVEL 3
All Short Vowels, Initial Consonant Clusters
sc-, sk-, sm-, sn-, sp-, st-, sw-
in CCVC Words

3. WORD READING

scat	smug	snug	spit	scum	skit
snap	spun	smog	swig	skid	slot
slat	slim	slam	sled	skim	stag
step	slip	snub	stun	swag	swot
slap	swop	snob	snag	stab	slab
scan	slop	swim	swam	skin	stem

SIGHT WORDS:

a	and	I
of	the	to
was	into	

4. SENTENCE READING

The stag did not slip in the fen.

I can not scan in the smog.

The skit was fun, and Stan was smug.

It is not fun to step in the scum.

Slap the mat on the slab.

The rat had a nap in the snug box.

Scat cat! Run in the sun.

Stan can swim in the dam.

A stem hit his leg and cut his skin.

Sam slid on his sled, and it was fun.

EXAMPLE #21 LESSON PLAN FOR LEVEL 3
All Short Vowels, Initial Consonant Clusters
sc-, sk-, sm-, sn-, sp-, st-, sw-
in CCVC Words

5. SPELLING WORDS

stem	skin	snug	swim	sled
slip	snug	scat	slid	snap

6. SENTENCE DICTATION

Snap the stem into six bits.

Stan slid on the sled.

Scat! Let me nap in a snug bed.

His skin is cut and has a red dot.

The mud is wet, and I can slip.

EXAMPLE #22 LESSON PLAN FOR LEVEL 3
Review All Short Vowels,
Review of All Initial Consonant Clusters
in CCVC Words

Student/Class: Date: Lesson #:

1. ALPHABET CARD DRILL

Reading Drill

Show the student one **Alphabet Drill Card** at a time. The student writes/traces the letter saying the letter(s) name(s), keyword and sound.

Use **Teacher Prompts** if necessary.

What is the name of this letter?

What is the keyword?

What is the sound this letter makes?

For Multiple Spellings Teacher Asks	Student Answers
What are the two sounds s makes?	*s snake /s/, s nose /z/*
What are the two sounds th makes?	*th thumb /th/, th there /th/*

a	b	c	d	e	f
g	h	i	j	k	l
m	n	o	p	qu	r
s and s₂	t	u	v	w	x
y	z	ch	ck	sh	th and th₂

EXAMPLE #22 LESSON PLAN FOR LEVEL 3
Review All Short Vowels,
Review of All Initial Consonant Clusters
in CCVC Words

 Spelling Drill

Do not show student each **Alphabet Drill Card** and ask:

What letter spells the sounds?

The teacher says the sound and the student traces/writes the letter(s)while saying the letter name(s), keyword and sound.

For Multiple Spellings Teacher Asks	Student Answers
How many ways can you spell /k/?	c, k, ck
How many ways can you spell /z/?	s, z

/ă/	/b/	/k/	/d/	/ĕ/	/f/
/g/	/h/	/ĭ/	/j/	/l/	/m/
/n/	/ŏ/	/p/	/kw/	/r/	/s/
/t/	/ŭ/	/v/	/w/	/ks/	/y/
/z/	/ch/	/sh/	/th/	/<u>th</u>/	

2. BLENDING

Use the **Initial Cluster Cards** and **Word Family Cards** in the **Appendix** and make real and nonsense words to be read aloud.

br	
cr	**an**
tr	

EXAMPLE #22 LESSON PLAN FOR LEVEL 3
Review All Short Vowels,
Review of All Initial Consonant Clusters
in CCVC Words

3. WORD READING

clap	glad	flex	prop	drum
cram	glen	from	plan	slap
brag	flip	glum	Fran	drop
clip	gram	bran	plod	slit
flat	glut	slid	slim	sled
twit	Brad	slam	slip	brag
stem	flan	fret	slop	flax
flag	flop	twin	slat	trip
scan	swim	skin	brim	clip
drop	twig	stun	sled	plum

SIGHT WORDS:

a	and	I
of	the	to
was	into	

EXAMPLE #22 LESSON PLAN FOR LEVEL 3
Review All Short Vowels,
Review of All Initial Consonant Clusters
in CCVC Words

SCOPE & SEQUENCE LEVELS 4-1 **S**

4. SENTENCE READING

The plan was to swim a lap at the dam.

The sled skid on the mud and did a flip.

Brad has a slim twin.

A frog can not hop on a stag.

A gram of bran is a not a lot of grub.

Bret is glum as his pal did not plan a trip.

His skin is red from the hot sun.

Plop the plum in the pot.

Slam the twig on the mat, and it can snap.

Fran is glad Trev the cat has a snug bed.

5. SPELLING WORDS

stem	twin	crab	plum	frog
flat	blot	skin	slap	twig

6. SENTENCE DICTATION

The twin has a pet frog.

Stan slid on wet twig.

Get a rag and blot up the wet slop.

I sat on the plum, and it is flat.

The flag had a crab on it.

GREAT WORD HOUSE
Reading & Spelling Program

EXAMPLE #23 LESSON PLAN FOR LEVEL 4
All Short Vowels, Clusters, Digraphs, Word Family *all*, with Suffix –*s*

Student/Class:	Date:	Lesson #:

NEW CONCEPT: The L Effect. When *ll* follows the letter *a* it changes the vowel sound to /aw/. *all* is a Word Family where the *a* is pronounced /aw/. Contrast *hat* with *hall*, *mat* with *mall*.

*Exception *shall*

1. ALPHABET CARD DRILL

 Reading Drill

Show the student one **Alphabet Drill Card** at a time. The student writes/traces the letter saying the letter(s) name(s), keyword and sound.

Use **Teacher Prompts** if necessary.

What is the name of this letter?

What is the keyword?

What is the sound this letter makes?

For Multiple Spellings Teacher Asks	Student Answers
What are the two sounds s makes?	*s snake /s/, s nose /z/*
What are the two sounds th makes?	*th thumb /th/, th there /th/*

a	b	c	d	e	f
g	h	i	j	k	l
m	n	o	p	qu	r
s and s₂	t	u	v	w	x
y	z	ch	ck	sh	th and th₂
all					

Page 105
greatwordhouse.com All rights reserved © 2018.

Spelling Drill

Do not show student each **Alphabet Drill Card** and ask:

What letter spells the sounds?

The teacher says the sound and the student traces/writes the letter(s)while saying the letter name(s), keyword and sound.

For Multiple Spellings Teacher Asks	Student Answers
How many ways can you spell /k/?	c, k, ck
How many ways can you spell /z/?	s, z

/ă/	/b/	/k/	/d/	/ě/	/f/
/g/	/h/	/ĭ/	/j/	/l/	/m/
/n/	/ŏ/	/p/	/kw/	/r/	/s/
/t/	/ŭ/	/v/	/w/	/ks/	/y/
/z/	/ch/	/sh/	/th/	/th̲/	/awl/

Suffix Drill

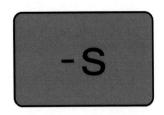

After the **Alphabet Card Drill**, tell the student that suffixes come at the end and are on red cards (red for 'stop'). The hyphen shows where the suffix is fixed or joined to the word.

Show the student the card and ask:

Teacher: *How do we know this is a suffix card?*

Student: *It is red and the letter has a hyphen in front.*

Teacher: *What does this hyphen show?*

Student: Where the word joins to it.

Teacher: *Please read the card.*

Student: *Suffix –s says /s/ and /z/.*

Teacher: *What are the jobs of suffix –s?*

Student: *It shows plural (more than one) e.g. cats, dogs. Suffix -s is used with he/she/it verbs, e.g. He digs. She sits. It yaps. Proper and common nouns can be used instead of he/she/it.*

EXAMPLE #23 LESSON PLAN FOR LEVEL 4
All Short Vowels, Clusters, Digraphs, Word Family *all*, with Suffix *–s*

2. BLENDING

b		
c		
d		
f		
g		
h		
m	**all**	**s**
p		
t		
w		
st		
sm		

3. WORD READING

ball	fall	tall	call	balls
mall	gall	hall	pall	falls
wall	small	stall	stalls	calls
malls	halls	walls	galls	palls

Contrast the vowel sounds in the word pairs below.					
mat	mall	cat	call	ham	hall
smack	small	fat	fall	gap	gall
pat	pall	wag	wall	stag	stall

SIGHT WORDS:

a	and	I
of	the	to
was	into	are
have	were	you

4. SENTENCE READING

The small balls fell from the sack.

A tall stag ran in the glen.

Stash the blocks in the hall.

Brad calls to his dog and cat.

In a flash, the fox got a small hen.

Jan will sell a red dress at the mall.

You can not stall, I have to get back at six.

The man at the stall had a lot of gall.

The sod was mud and the wall fell.

A pall of black smog fell as I ran up the path.

5. SPELLING WORDS

ball	call	hall	mall	tall
fall	wall	pall	stall	small

6. SENTENCE DICTATION

I got a bag of plums at the stall.

In the hall, Brad will sell a ball.

The small rat ran to the tall dog.

Pat got a black top and a red dress at the mall.

A tall lad got a call on his cell.

GREAT WORD HOUSE ™
Reading & Spelling Program

EXAMPLE #24 LESSON PLAN FOR LEVEL 4
Short Vowels with *ng* and *n₂*
in CVCC and CCVCC Words.

Student/Class: Date: Lesson #:

NEW CONCEPT: End Cluster –*nk* is found at the end of a word. The letter *n* has a second sound (n_2) when it is in front of *k*, e.g. *rink*. The sound of *n* changes as the regular sound is hard say. Ask the student to try and say *rink* with the regular sound of *n*. It will be difficult! The sound of n_2 is represented with this symbol which looks like a combination of *n* and *g*, /ŋ/.

NEW CONCEPT: The digraph *ng* also makes the sound /ŋ/. This digraph never appears at the beginning of a word only in the middle and the end, e.g. *ring*.

1. ALPHABET CARD DRILL

Reading Drill

Show the student one **Alphabet Drill Card** at a time. The student writes/traces the letter saying the letter(s) name(s), keyword and sound.
Use **Teacher Prompts** if necessary.

What is the name of this letter?
What is the keyword?
What is the sound this letter makes?

For Multiple Spellings Teacher Asks	Student Answers
What are the two sounds s makes?	*s snake /s/, s nose /z/*
What are the two sounds th makes?	*th thumb /th/, th there /th/*
What are the two sounds n makes?	*n net /n/ and n rink /ŋ/*

a	b	c	d	e	f
g	h	i	j	k	l
m	n and n₂	o	p	qu	r
s and s₂	t	u	v	w	x
y	z	ch	ck	sh	th and th₂
all	ng				

EXAMPLE #24 LESSON PLAN FOR LEVEL 4
Short Vowels with *ng* and *n₂* in CVCC and CCVCC Words.

 Spelling Drill

Do not show student each **Alphabet Drill Card** and ask:

What letter spells the sounds?

The teacher says the sound and the student traces/writes the letter(s)while saying the letter name(s), keyword and sound.

For Multiple Spellings Teacher Asks	Student Answers
How many ways can you spell /k/?	*c, k, ck*
How many ways can you spell /z/?	*s, z*
How many ways can you spell /ŋ/?	*n, ng*

/ă/	/b/	/k/	/d/	/ĕ/	/f/
/g/	/h/	/ĭ/	/j/	/l/	/m/
/n/ and /ŋ/	/ŏ/	/p/	/kw/	/r/	/s/
/t/	/ŭ/	/v/	/w/	/ks/	/y/
/z/	/ch/	/sh/	/th/ and /th/	/awl/	

EXAMPLE #24 LESSON PLAN FOR LEVEL 4
Short Vowels with *ng* and *n₂*
in CVCC and CCVCC Words.

2. BLENDING

b	**a**nk
bl	
c	
cl	**a**ng
d	
dr	**i**nk
f	
fl	**o**nk
h	
l	
m	**o**ng
p	
pl	**u**nk
t	
w	
sl	**u**ng
st	
sw	**i**ng

*Avoid creating the word *monk*. It is an exception word as the o sounds like short *u* /ŭ/.

EXAMPLE #24 LESSON PLAN FOR LEVEL 4
Short Vowels with *ng* and *n₂*
in CVCC and CCVCC Words.

3. WORD READING

bank	link	honk	bang	flung	fling
blank	mink	bunk	clang	stung	king
dank	pink	clunk	gang	bong	ping
flank	plink	dunk	hang	dong	ring
lank	sink	hunk	pang	gong	sing
prank	stink	junk	rang	long	sling
rank	slink	plunk	sang	pong	sting
sank	wink	sunk	slang	song	swing
stank	chink	stunk	bung	bing	ting
spank	blink	drunk	hung	cling	thing
swank	drink	chunk	ding	bring	wing
yank	clink	swung	slung	bling	sung

SIGHT WORDS:

a	and	I
of	the	to
was	into	are
have	were	you

EXAMPLE #24 LESSON PLAN FOR LEVEL 4
Short Vowels with *ng* and n_2
in CVCC and CCVCC Words.

GREAT WORD HOUSE
Reading & Spelling Program

4. SENTENCE READING

The bell rang with a ting.

A pink mink sung a long song.

Bing bong sang the gong.

The gang did not rob a bank.

The jet had a long wing.

If you step in the mud, you will sink.

With a honk, the duck swam off.

A bug stung Mick on his leg.

The king hung a mink cloth on his neck.

The club has fun at that rink.

5. SPELLING WORDS

sink	bank	honk	think	junk
ring	sing	long	wing	bang
stink	blank	trunk	blink	spunk
bring	sling	prong	swing	thing

EXAMPLE #24 LESSON PLAN FOR LEVEL 4
Short Vowels with *ng* and *n₂*
in CVCC and CCVCC Words.

GREAT WORD HOUSE
Reading & Spelling Program

6. SENTENCE DICTATION

The cups and dishes are in the sink.

I have a small bit of cash in the bank.

Ross slung the junk in the bin.

Can you think of a thing that can ring?

That smell is a big stink.

EXAMPLE #25 LESSON PLAN FOR LEVEL 4
Short Vowels with *ng* and *n₂* in CVCC, CCVCC Words and Suffix *-s*

Student/Class: _____   Date: _____   Lesson #: _____

1. ALPHABET CARD DRILL

Reading Drill

Show the student one **Alphabet Drill Card** at a time. The student writes/traces the letter saying the letter(s) name(s), keyword and sound.

Use **Teacher Prompts** if necessary.

What is the name of this letter?

What is the keyword?

What is the sound this letter makes?

For Multiple Spellings Teacher Asks	Student Answers
What are the two sounds s makes?	*s snake /s/, s nose /z/*
What are the two sounds th makes?	*th thumb /th/, th there /th/*
What are the two sounds n makes?	*n net /n/ and n rink /ŋ/*

a	b	c	d	e	f
g	h	i	j	k	l
m	n and n₂	o	p	qu	r
s and s₂	t	u	v	w	x
y	z	ch	ck	sh	th and th₂
all	ng				

EXAMPLE #25 LESSON PLAN FOR LEVEL 4
Short Vowels with *ng* and *n*₂
in CVCC, CCVCC Words and Suffix *-s*

 Spelling Drill

Do not show student each **Alphabet Drill Card** and ask:

What letter spells the sounds?

The teacher says the sound and the student traces/writes the letter(s) while saying the letter name(s), keyword and sound.

For Multiple Spellings Teacher Asks	Student Answers
How many ways can you spell /k/?	c, k, ck
How many ways can you spell /z/?	s, z
How many ways can you spell /ŋ/?	n, ng

/ă/	/b/	/k/	/d/	/ĕ/	/f/
/g/	/h/	/ĭ/	/j/	/l/	/m/
/n/ and /ŋ/	/ŏ/	/p/	/kw/	/r/	/s/
/t/	/ŭ/	/v/	/w/	/ks/	/y/
/z/	/ch/	/sh/	/th/ and /<u>th</u>/	/awl/	

EXAMPLE #25 LESSON PLAN FOR LEVEL 4
Short Vowels with *ng* and *n₂*
in CVCC, CCVCC Words and Suffix *-s*

Suffix Drill

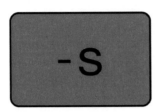

After the **Alphabet Card Drill**, tell the student that suffixes come at the end and are on red cards (red for 'stop'). The hyphen shows where the suffix is fixed or joined to the word.

Show the student the card and ask:

Teacher: *How do we know this is a suffix card?*

Student: *It is red and the letter has a hyphen in front.*

Teacher: *What does this hyphen show?*

Student: Where the word joins to it.

Teacher: *Please read the card.*

Student: *Suffix –s says /s/ and /z/.*

Teacher: *What are the jobs of suffix –s?*

Student: *It shows plural (more than one) e.g. cats, dogs. Suffix -s is used with he/she/it verbs, e.g. He digs. She sits. It yaps. Proper and common nouns can be used instead of he/she/it.*

EXAMPLE #25 LESSON PLAN FOR LEVEL 4
Short Vowels with *ng* and *n*$_2$
in CVCC, CCVCC Words and Suffix *-s*

GREAT
WORD
HOUSE
Reading & Spelling
Program

SCOPE & SEQUENCE
S
LEVELS 1-4

2. BLENDING

b	ank	
bl		
c	ang	
cl		
d		
dr	ink	
f		
fl	onk	
h		s
l		
m	ong	
p		
pl	unk	
t		
w	ung	
sl		
st	ing	
sw		

*Avoid creating the word *monk*. It is an exception word as the o sounds like short *u* /ŭ/.

EXAMPLE #25 LESSON PLAN FOR LEVEL 4
Short Vowels with *ng* and *n*$_2$
in CVCC, CCVCC Words and Suffix *-s*

3. WORD READING

banks	links	bangs	honks
blanks	minks	fangs	longs
flanks	sinks	gangs	gongs
pranks	stinks	thongs	tongs
spanks	slinks	hangs	songs
swanks	chinks	sings	wings
bunks	blinks	rings	stings
hunks	drinks	kings	slings
chunks	clinks	bongs	flings
plunks	thinks	clings	clangs
thinks	clanks	things	bungs
winks	planks	brings	pings
yanks	cranks	swings	dings

SIGHT WORDS:

a	**and**	**I**
of	**the**	**to**
was	**into**	**are**
have	**were**	**you**

EXAMPLE #25 LESSON PLAN FOR LEVEL 4
Short Vowels with *ng* and *n*$_2$
in CVCC, CCVCC Words and Suffix *-s*

4. SENTENCE READING

The bell rings with six tings and ten bongs.

The king sings lots of songs.

Chunks of rock fell on the banks of the dam.

The things in the bags are gongs.

The mad bats have wings and fangs.

Chet thinks that his van clanks a lot.

Sam blinks in the black smog that stinks.

Ben yanks his bag with prongs, but it is stuck.

With long honks, the ducks swam off.

My leg has a red spot and it stings.

5. SPELLING WORDS

sinks	banks	honks	thinks	hunks
rings	sings	longs	wings	bangs
stinks	blanks	trunks	blinks	dunks
brings	slings	prongs	swings	things

EXAMPLE #25 LESSON PLAN FOR LEVEL 4
Short Vowels with *ng* and *n₂*
in CVCC, CCVCC Words and Suffix *-s*

6. SENTENCE DICTATION

Jan brings lots of things to class.

The bog stinks in the hot sun.

Ben sings to all the kings.

The men nap on bunks.

The rings fell from the bag with clanks and clinks.

EXAMPLE #26 LESSON PLAN FOR LEVEL 4
Soft Sounds of *C* and *G* in Final Position
(1st job of Silent **e**) in VCCe Words.

GREAT WORD HOUSE
Reading & Spelling
Program

Student/Class: Date: Lesson #:

NEW CONCEPT: When *c* and *g* are followed by *e*, these letters become "soft". Soft *c* (c_2) sounds like /s/. Soft *g* (g_2) sounds like /j/. This is also known as the **First Job of Silent e.**

1. ALPHABET CARD DRILL

Reading Drill

Show the student one **Alphabet Drill Card** at a time. The student writes/traces the letter saying the letter(s) name(s), keyword and sound.

Use **Teacher Prompts** if necessary.

What is the name of this letter?

What is the keyword?

What is the sound this letter makes?

For Multiple Spellings Teacher Asks	Student Answers
What are the two sounds s makes?	*s snake /s/, s nose /z/*
What are the two sounds c makes?	*c cat /k/, c dance /s/*
What are the two sounds g makes?	*g goat /g/, g hinge /j/*
What are the two sounds th makes?	*th thumb /th/, th there /th/*
What are the two sounds n makes?	*n net /n/ and n rink /ŋ/*

a	b	c and c_2	d	e	f
g and g_2	h	i	j	k	l
m	n and n_2	o	p	qu	r
s and s_2	t	u	v	w	x
y	z	ch	ck	sh	th and th_2
all	ng				

GREAT WORD HOUSE
Reading & Spelling Program

EXAMPLE #26 LESSON PLAN FOR LEVEL 4
Soft Sounds of *C* and *G* in Final Position
(1st job of Silent *e*) in VCCe Words.

 Spelling Drill

Do not show student each **Alphabet Drill Card** and ask:

What letter spells the sounds?

The teacher says the sound and the student traces/writes the letter(s)while saying the letter name(s), keyword and sound.

For Multiple Spellings Teacher Asks	Student Answers
How many ways can you spell /k/?	c, k, ck
How many ways can you spell /z/?	s, z
How many ways can you spell /s/?	c, s
How many ways can you spell /j/?	g, j
How many ways can you spell /ŋ/?	n, ng

/ă/	/b/	/k/	/d/	/ĕ/	/f/
/g/	/h/	/ĭ/	/j/	/l/	/m/
/n/ and /ŋ/	/ŏ/	/p/	/kw/	/r/	/s/
/t/	/ŭ/	/v/	/w/	/ks/	/y/
/z/	/ch/	/sh/	/th/ and /<u>th</u>/	/awl/	

EXAMPLE #26 LESSON PLAN FOR LEVEL 4
Soft Sounds of *C* and *G* in Final Position
(1st job of Silent **e**) in VCCe Words.

2. BLENDING

dan		bin	
fen		bul	
hen		hin	
glan		plun	
lan		crin	
prin		frin	
pran	ce	frin	ge
min		flan	
stan		lun	
chan		sin	
sin		grun	
tran		tin	
win		twin	
quin			

3. WORD READING

dance	prince	hinge	lunge
lance	quince	singe	plunge
chance	mince	tinge	grunge
prance	since	twinge	bulge
stance	hence	cringe	flange
trance	fence	binge	fringe
glance	sconce	dunce	henge

EXAMPLE #26 LESSON PLAN FOR LEVEL 4
Soft Sounds of *C* and *G* in Final Position
(1st job of Silent e) in VCCe Words.

SIGHT WORDS:

a	and	I
of	the	to
was	into	are
have	were	you

4. SENTENCE READING

Stan had a twinge in his back.

I had quince and mince in my lunch tin.

The prince is in a trance.

The flange of the hinge has a ding.

Chant and dance and you will not get sad.

If you singe the ham, dad will get cross.

Mom will cringe at the mess in the den.

Plunge in and swim a bit.

I met Dan by chance at the fence.

The fringe of the rug has a tinge of red.

5. SPELLING WORDS

dance	prince	lance	mince	chance
fringe	hinge	tinge	lunge	cringe

EXAMPLE #26 LESSON PLAN FOR LEVEL 4
Soft Sounds of *C* and *G* in Final Position (1st job of Silent e) in VCCe Words.

6. SENTENCE DICTATION

The prince is at the dance.

Get a hinge and fix it on the cat flap.

I can not lunge as my leg is stiff.

Lance has got a chance to win.

If the boss yells, I cringe.

EXAMPLE #27 LESSON PLAN FOR LEVEL 4
Soft Sounds of *C* and *G* in Final Position in VCCe Words and Suffix *–es*

Student/Class: _____ **Date:** _____ **Lesson #:** _____

NEW CONCEPT: Suffix *-es* is a vowel suffix as it begins with a vowel. For words ending in *ce* and *ge*, add the suffix *–es* and drop the **Silent e**.
See **GWH Spelling Rule Book** for further information and exercises.
Drop the Silent e: When a word ends in a Silent e, drop the *e* when adding a vowel suffix. For example, *dance + ing = dancing*

1. ALPHABET CARD DRILL

Reading Drill

Show the student one **Alphabet Drill Card** at a time. The student writes/traces the letter saying the letter(s) name(s), keyword and sound.
Use **Teacher Prompts** if necessary.

What is the name of this letter?
What is the keyword?
What is the sound this letter makes?

For Multiple Spellings Teacher Asks	Student Answers
What are the two sounds s makes?	*s snake /s/, s nose /z/*
What are the two sounds c makes?	*c cat /k/, c dance /s/*
What are the two sounds g makes?	*g goat /g/, g hinge /j/*
What are the two sounds th makes?	*th thumb /th/, th there /th/*
What are the two sounds n makes?	*n net /n/ and n rink /ŋ/*

a	b	c and c$_2$	d	e	f
g and g$_2$	h	i	j	k	l
m	n and n$_2$	o	p	qu	r
s and s$_2$	t	u	v	w	x
y	z	ch	ck	sh	th and th$_2$
all	ng				

EXAMPLE #27 LESSON PLAN FOR LEVEL 4

Soft Sounds of *C* and *G* in Final Position in VCCe Words and Suffix –*es*

 Spelling Drill

Do not show student each **Alphabet Drill Card** and ask:

What letter spells the sounds?

The teacher says the sound and the student traces/writes the letter(s)while saying the letter name(s), keyword and sound.

For Multiple Spellings Teacher Asks	Student Answers
How many ways can you spell /k/?	*c, k, ck*
How many ways can you spell /z/?	*s, z*
How many ways can you spell /s/?	*c, s*
How many ways can you spell /j/?	*g, j*
How many ways can you spell /ŋ/?	*n, ng*

/ă/	/b/	/k/	/d/	/ĕ/	/f/
/g/	/h/	/ĭ/	/j/	/l/	/m/
/n/ and /ŋ/	/ŏ/	/p/	/kw/	/r/	/s/
/t/	/ŭ/	/v/	/w/	/ks/	/y/
/z/	/ch/	/sh/	/th/ and /<u>th</u>/	/awl/	

Suffix Drill

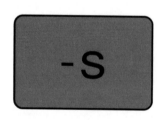

Teacher: *Please read the cards.*

Student: *–s says /s/ and /z/; -es says /əz/.*

Teacher: *What are the jobs of suffix –s and –es?*

Student: *They show plural (more than one), e.g. cats, kisses. They are used with he/she/it verbs, e.g. He digs. She sits. It yaps. He fishes. She rushes. It messes. Proper and common nouns can be used instead of he/she/it.*

GREAT
WORD
HOUSE
Reading & Spelling
Program

EXAMPLE #27 LESSON PLAN FOR LEVEL 4
Soft Sounds of *C* and *G* in Final Position
in VCCe Words and Suffix *–es*

2. BLENDING

dance		binge	
fence		bulge	
glance		hinge	
lance		plunge	
prince	**es**	cringe	**es**
prance		fringe	
mince		flange	
chance		lunge	
trance		singe	
wince		tinge	
quince		twinge	

3. WORD READING

dances	princes	hinges	lunges
lances	quinces	singes	plunges
chances	mince	tinges	blanches
prances	fences	twinges	bulges
stances	glances	cringes	flanges
trances	dunces	binges	fringes

SIGHT WORDS:

a	and	I
of	the	to
was	into	are
have	were	you

EXAMPLE #27 LESSON PLAN FOR LEVEL 4
Soft Sounds of *C* and *G* in Final Position in VCC*e* Words and Suffix *–es*

4. SENTENCE READING

Stan had twinges in his back.

I had quinces in my lunch tin.

The princes have fun at the dances.

I sell brass hinges at my stall.

Pam plunges cod in the pot and singes it.

Mom cringes at the mess in the den.

The chances of a win are small.

Fix the fences and the fox will not get in.

The fringes of the rug have lots of mud.

In his top hat, Brad got lots of glances.

5. SPELLING WORDS

dances	princes	glances	quinces	chances
fringes	hinges	singes	lunges	cringes

6. SENTENCE DICTATION

The princes got glances at the dance.

The cat flap has brass hinges.

The chances are slim that I will win.

If mom yells, the lad cringes.

Dad singes the quinces in the pot.

EXAMPLE #28 LESSON PLAN FOR LEVEL 4
Quiet End Clusters in
CVCC, CCVCC Words

Student/Class: **Date:**   **Lesson #:**

1. ALPHABET CARD DRILL

Reading Drill

Show the student one **Alphabet Drill Card** at a time. The student writes/ traces the letter saying the letter(s) name(s), keyword and sound.

Use **Teacher Prompts** if necessary.

What is the name of this letter?

What is the keyword?

What is the sound this letter makes?

For Multiple Spellings Teacher Asks	Student Answers
What are the two sounds s makes?	*s snake /s/, s nose /z/*
What are the two sounds c makes?	*c cat /k/, c dance /s/*
What are the two sounds g makes?	*g goat /g/, g hinge /j/*
What are the two sounds th makes?	*th thumb /th/, th there /th/*
What are the two sounds n makes?	*n net /n/ and n rink /ŋ/*

a	b	c and c$_2$	d	e	f
g and g$_2$	h	i	j	k	l
m	n and n$_2$	o	p	qu	r
s and s$_2$	t	u	v	w	x
y	z	ch	ck	sh	th and th$_2$
all	ng				

EXAMPLE #28 LESSON PLAN FOR LEVEL 4
Quiet End Clusters in
CVCC, CCVCC Words

Spelling Drill

Do not show student each **Alphabet Drill Card** and ask:

What letter spells the sounds?

The teacher says the sound and the student traces/writes the letter(s)while saying the letter name(s), keyword and sound.

For Multiple Spellings Teacher Asks	Student Answers
How many ways can you spell /k/?	c, k, ck
How many ways can you spell /z/?	s, z
How many ways can you spell /s/?	c, s
How many ways can you spell /j/?	g, j
How many ways can you spell /ŋ/?	n, ng

/ă/	/b/	/k/	/d/	/ĕ/	/f/
/g/	/h/	/ĭ/	/j/	/l/	/m/
/n/ and /ŋ/	/ŏ/	/p/	/kw/	/r/	/s/
/t/	/ŭ/	/v/	/w/	/ks/	/y/
/z/	/ch/	/sh/	/th/ and /<u>th</u>/	/awl/	

2. BLENDING

g	asp
b	est
l	ist
w	isp
ch	est
n	ext
t	usk
p	act
s	ect
s	ift
r	apt
k	ept
m	ust
l	ost

EXAMPLE #28 LESSON PLAN FOR LEVEL 4
Quiet End Clusters in CVCC, CCVCC Words

3. WORD READING

VCC	CVCC	CVCC	CCVCC
act	gasp	fact	clasp
aft	hasp	pact	grasp
ask	rasp	tact	crisp
asp	lisp	*gift	crept
apt	wisp	lift	tract
opt	Copt	rift	blast
oft	rapt	sift	chest
	kept	deft	crest
	wept	left	quest
	cast	weft	crust
	fast	loft	trust
	vast	soft	twist
	best	tuft	craft
	jest	dusk	draft
	lest	husk	shaft
	pest	musk	shift
	rest	rusk	drift
	test	tusk	croft
	vest	bask	brisk
	west	cask	whisk
	zest	mask	whist
	bust	task	
	dust	desk	
	gust	disk	
	just	risk	
	must	next	
	rust	disc	
	list		
	mist	*Hard g	

SIGHT WORDS:

a	and	I
of	the	to
was	into	are
have	were	you

4. SENTENCE READING

I must ask Tim to fix his desk.

It is a risk to lift that chest.

Mick is fast at chess and the best.

I wept at the list of jobs I got.

Pam had a rest and got up with zest.

At dusk, I crept into bed.

Mom kept a rusk in the tin.

I went for a brisk jog in the mist.

The loft has a lot of dust.

Len had to shift his desk.

5. SPELLING WORDS

gift	west	fact	ask	chest
must	trust	risk	next	twist

6. SENTENCE DICTATION

Ask the next cab if we can get a lift.

In the chest is a gift.

The blast left the mast with a twist.

I can not grasp that fact.

It is not a risk as I trust them.

EXAMPLE #29 LESSON PLAN FOR LEVEL 4
Quiet End Clusters with Suffix *–s*
in CVCC and CCVCC Words

Student/Class: **Date:**   **Lesson #:**

1. ALPHABET CARD DRILL

 Reading Drill

Show the student one **Alphabet Drill Card** at a time. The student writes/ traces the letter saying the letter(s) name(s), keyword and sound.

Use **Teacher Prompts** if necessary.

What is the name of this letter?

What is the keyword?

What is the sound this letter makes?

For Multiple Spellings Teacher Asks	Student Answers
What are the two sounds s makes?	*s snake /s/, s nose /z/*
What are the two sounds c makes?	*c cat /k/, c dance /s/*
What are the two sounds g makes?	*g goat /g/, g hinge /j/*
What are the two sounds th makes?	*th thumb /th/, th there /th/*
What are the two sounds n makes?	*n net /n/ and n rink /ŋ/*

a	b	c and c$_2$	d	e	f
g and g$_2$	h	i	j	k	l
m	n and n$_2$	o	p	qu	r
s and s$_2$	t	u	v	w	x
y	z	ch	ck	sh	th and th$_2$
all	ng				

 Spelling Drill

Do not show student each **Alphabet Drill Card** and ask:

What letter spells the sounds?

The teacher says the sound and the student traces/writes the letter(s)while saying the letter name(s), keyword and sound.

For Multiple Spellings Teacher Asks	Student Answers
How many ways can you spell /k/?	c, k, ck
How many ways can you spell /z/?	s, z
How many ways can you spell /s/?	c, s
How many ways can you spell /j/?	g, j
How many ways can you spell /ŋ/?	n, ng

/ă/	/b/	/k/	/d/	/ĕ/	/f/
/g/	/h/	/ĭ/	/j/	/l/	/m/
/n/ and /ŋ/	/ŏ/	/p/	/kw/	/r/	/s/
/t/	/ŭ/	/v/	/w/	/ks/	/y/
/z/	/ch/	/sh/	/th/ and /<u>th</u>/	/awl/	

Suffix Drill

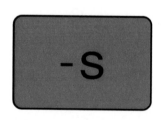

Teacher: *Please read the cards.*

Student: *–s says /s/ and /z/.*

Teacher: *What are the jobs of suffix –s?*

Student: *They show plural (more than one), e.g. cats.. They are used with he/she/it verbs, e.g. He digs. She sits. It yaps. Proper and common nouns can be used instead of he/she/it.*

EXAMPLE #29 LESSON PLAN FOR LEVEL 4
Quiet End Clusters with Suffix –s
in CVCC and CCVCC Words

SCOPE & SEQUENCE
S
LEVELS 1-4

2. BLENDING

gasp_	test_	list_	wisp_	chest_
tusk_	gulf_	pact_	cost_	craft_
gift_	mist_	loft_	husk_	trust_
ask_	cast_	sift_	vest_	shift_
fact_	mask_	pact_	quest_	gasp_
tuft_	sect_	risk_	lift_	tract_
rust_	pest_	rasp_	lisp_	twist_

3. WORD READING

VCC	CVCC	CVCC	CCVCC
acts	gasps	facts	clasps
asks	hasps	pacts	grasps
asps	rasps	*gifts	crisps
opts	lisps	lifts	tracts
	wisps	rifts	blasts
	Copts	sifts	chests
	casts	lofts	crests
	jests	tufts	quests
	pests	tasks	crusts
	rests	husks	trusts
	tests	rusks	twists
	vests	tusks	crafts
	busts	basks	drafts
	dusts	casks	shafts
	gusts	masks	shifts
	rusts	desks	drifts
	lists	disks	crofts
	mists	risks	whisks
		discs	
		*Hard g	

EXAMPLE #29 LESSON PLAN FOR LEVEL 4
Quiet End Clusters with Suffix –s
in CVCC and CCVCC Words

SIGHT WORDS:

a	and	I
of	the	to
was	into	are
have	were	you

4. SENTENCE READING

Tim asks Tom to fix the desks.

Kim gasps at the risks.

Mick trusts that the van will run.

The boss grasps the lists of tasks.

Pam rests and Jim acts.

The hog digs with his tusks.

Dad kept his rusks in a box.

In the chests were lots of crafts.

The cat basks in the sun.

Len had six shifts in the shop.

EXAMPLE #29 LESSON PLAN FOR LEVEL 4
Quiet End Clusters with Suffix –s
in CVCC and CCVCC Words

5. SPELLING WORDS

gifts	masks	facts	asks	shifts
clasps	trusts	risks	lofts	twists

6. SENTENCE DICTATION

In the chests are lots of gifts.

Jack asks if Jim trusts him.

Fran shifts and twists on the mat.

I had six tests on my math facts.

The cast had masks on.

EXAMPLE #30 LESSON PLAN FOR LEVEL 4
Noisy, Noisy & Quiet End Clusters in CVCC and CCVCC Words

Student/Class: Date: Lesson #:

1. ALPHABET CARD DRILL

 Reading Drill

Show the student one **Alphabet Drill Card** at a time. The student writes/ traces the letter saying the letter(s) name(s), keyword and sound.

Use **Teacher Prompts** if necessary.

What is the name of this letter?

What is the keyword?

What is the sound this letter makes?

For Multiple Spellings Teacher Asks	Student Answers
What are the two sounds s makes?	*s snake /s/, s nose /z/*
What are the two sounds c makes?	*c cat /k/, c dance /s/*
What are the two sounds g makes?	*g goat /g/, g hinge /j/*
What are the two sounds th makes?	*th thumb /th/, th there /th/*
What are the two sounds n makes?	*n net /n/ and n rink /ŋ/*

a	b	c and c$_2$	d	e	f
g and g$_2$	h	i	j	k	l
m	n and n$_2$	o	p	qu	r
s and s$_2$	t	u	v	w	x
y	z	ch	ck	sh	th and th$_2$
all	ng				

EXAMPLE #30 LESSON PLAN FOR LEVEL 4
Noisy, Noisy & Quiet End Clusters in CVCC and CCVCC Words

 Spelling Drill

Do not show student each **Alphabet Drill Card** and ask:

What letter spells the sounds?

The teacher says the sound and the student traces/writes the letter(s)while saying the letter name(s), keyword and sound.

For Multiple Spellings Teacher Asks	Student Answers
How many ways can you spell /k/?	*c, k, ck*
How many ways can you spell /z/?	*s, z*
How many ways can you spell /s/?	*c, s*
How many ways can you spell /j/?	*g, j*
How many ways can you spell /ŋ/?	*n, ng*

/ă/	/b/	/k/	/d/	/ĕ/	/f/
/g/	/h/	/ĭ/	/j/	/l/	/m/
/n/ and /ŋ/	/ŏ/	/p/	/kw/	/r/	/s/
/t/	/ŭ/	/v/	/w/	/ks/	/y/
/z/	/ch/	/sh/	/th/ and /th/	/awl/	

EXAMPLE #30 LESSON PLAN FOR LEVEL 4
Noisy, Noisy & Quiet End Clusters in CVCC and CCVCC Words

2. BLENDING

l	amp
h	ump
b	and
s	end
l	ink
w	ent
h	eld
sh	elf
h	ulk
h	elm
h	elp
s	ilt
br	and
cl	amp
j	inx

3. WORD READING

VCC	CVCC	CVCC	CCVCC	VCCC
alp	camp	helm	champ	kempt
amp	damp	held	chimp	tempt
and	lamp	meld	chump	midst
ant	ramp	weld	thump	
elf	limp	help	chant	
elk	wimp	gulp	shunt	
elm	dump	kilt	shalt	
ilk	hump	silt	thank	
imp	lump	wilt	think	
ink	pump	milk	shank	
	band	silk	crank	
	hand	kink	plank	
	land	link	plink	
	sand	mink	plonk	
	bend	pink	clamp	
	lend	sink	clump	
	send	wink	plump	
	tend	hunk	slump	
	fond	bank	cramp	
	pond	dank	tramp	
	fund	lank	trump	
	pant	sank	shelf	
	rant	tank	brand	
	cent	yank	grand	
	gent	dunk	blend	
	lent	sunk	spend	
	rent	jinx	trend	
	tent	minx	stand	

3. WORD READING CONTINUED

VCC	CVCC	CVCC	CCVCC	VCCC
	font		blond	
	hunt		frond	
			grant	
			plant	
			slant	
			blunt	
			brunt	
			grunt	
			stunt	
			skunk	

SIGHT WORDS:

a	and	I
of	the	to
was	into	are
have	were	you

4. SENTENCE READING

Len can dip his hand in the pond.

Mom held my hand as I had a limp.

I will gulp a glass of milk.

The camp has just one tent.

You can not hunt on that land.

The brand has a pink skunk on it.

You can thank that grand man.

It is a trend to spend a lot on rent.

Think of a plan to fix that stand.

Can you tempt that chimp to sit on a bench?

5. SPELLING WORDS

milk	send	hunt	land	fond
champ	grant	plant	think	shelf

6. SENTENCE DICTATION

I am fond of milk.

Send them the rent.

The king will grant one wish.

I will plant cobs on the land.

Stan is a champ at chess.

EXAMPLE #31 LESSON PLAN FOR LEVEL 4
Noisy, Noisy & Quiet End Clusters in CVCC and CCVCC Words with
Suffix *-s* /s/, *-s* /z/ and *-es* /əz/

Student/Class: **Date:**   **Lesson #:**

1. ALPHABET CARD DRILL

 Reading Drill

Show the student one **Alphabet Drill Card** at a time. The student writes/ traces the letter saying the letter(s) name(s), keyword and sound.

Use **Teacher Prompts** if necessary.

What is the name of this letter?

What is the keyword?

What is the sound this letter makes?

For Multiple Spellings Teacher Asks	Student Answers
What are the two sounds s makes?	*s snake /s/, s nose /z/*
What are the two sounds c makes?	*c cat /k/, c dance /s/*
What are the two sounds g makes?	*g goat /g/, g hinge /j/*
What are the two sounds th makes?	*th thumb /th/, th there /th/*
What are the two sounds n makes?	*n net /n/ and n rink /ŋ/*

a	b	c and c₂	d	e	f
g and g₂	h	i	j	k	l
m	n and n₂	o	p	qu	r
s and s₂	t	u	v	w	x
y	z	ch	ck	sh	th and th₂
all	ng				

Note: "c and c₂", "g and g₂", "n and n₂", "s and s₂", "th and th₂" contain subscript 2 written as c_2, g_2, n_2, s_2, th_2.

EXAMPLE #31 LESSON PLAN FOR LEVEL 4
Noisy, Noisy & Quiet End Clusters in CVCC and CCVCC Words with
Suffix -s /s/, -s /z/ and -es /əz/

Spelling Drill

Do not show student each **Alphabet Drill Card** and ask:

   What letter spells the sounds?

The teacher says the sound and the student traces/writes the letter(s)while saying the letter name(s), keyword and sound.

For Multiple Spellings Teacher Asks	Student Answers
How many ways can you spell /k/?	c, k, ck
How many ways can you spell /z/?	s, z
How many ways can you spell /s/?	c, s
How many ways can you spell /j/?	g, j
How many ways can you spell /ŋ/?	n, ng

/ă/	/b/	/k/	/d/	/ĕ/	/f/
/g/	/h/	/ĭ/	/j/	/l/	/m/
/n/ and /ŋ/	/ŏ/	/p/	/kw/	/r/	/s/
/t/	/ŭ/	/v/	/w/	/ks/	/y/
/z/	/ch/	/sh/	/th/ and /<u>th</u>/	/awl/	

Suffix Drill

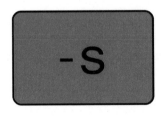

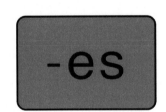

Teacher: *Please read the cards.*
Student: *–s says /s/ and /z/; -es says /əz/.*
Teacher: *What are the jobs of suffix –s and –es?*
Student: *They show plural (more than one), e.g. cats, kisses. They are used with he/she/it verbs, e.g. He digs. She sits. It yaps. He fishes. She rushes. It messes. Proper and common nouns can be used instead of he/she/it.*

EXAMPLE #31 LESSON PLAN FOR LEVEL 4

Noisy, Noisy & Quiet End Clusters in CVCC and CCVCC Words with Suffix *-s /s/*, *-s /z/* and *-es /əz/*

SCOPE & SEQUENCE
S
LEVELS 1-4

2. BLENDING

lamp	
hand	
hump	
band	
send	
link	s (quiet)
pond	
hulk	
help	s (noisy)
wilt	
thank	
chimp	
clamp	es
shunt	
thump	
weld	
elm	
jinx	
lens	
tempt	

EXAMPLE #31 LESSON PLAN FOR LEVEL 4
Noisy, Noisy & Quiet End Clusters in CVCC and CCVCC Words with
Suffix *-s* /s/, *-s* /z/ and *-es* /əz/

3. WORD READING

Nouns and verbs with suffix -s

VCC	CVCC	CVCC	CCVCC	VCCC
alps	camps	melds	champs	tempts
amps	lamps	welds	chimps	
ants	ramps	helps	chumps	
elks	limps	gulps	thumps	
elms	wimps	kilts	chants	
imps	dumps	wilts	shunts	
inks	humps	milks	thanks	
	lumps	silks	thinks	
	pumps	kinks	shanks	
	bands	links	cranks	
	hands	minks	planks	
	lands	sinks	plinks	
	sands	winks	plonks	
	bends	hunks	clamps	
	lends	banks	clumps	
	sends	tanks	plumps	
	tends	yanks	slumps	
	ponds	dunks	cramps	
	funds	jinxes	tramps	
	pants	minxes	brands	
	rants	lenses	glands	
	cents		blends	
	gents		spends	
	rents		trends	
	tents		stands	
	fonts		fronds	

EXAMPLE #31 LESSON PLAN FOR LEVEL 4
Noisy, Noisy & Quiet End Clusters in CVCC and CCVCC Words with Suffix *-s* /s/, *-s* /z/ and *-es* /əz/

3. WORD READING CONTINUED

Nouns and verbs with suffix -s

VCC	CVCC	CVCC	CCVCC	VCCC
	hunts		grants	
			plants	
			slants	
			blunts	
			grunts	
			stunts	
			skunks	

SIGHT WORDS:

a	and	I
of	the	to
was	into	are
have	were	you

EXAMPLE #31 LESSON PLAN FOR LEVEL 4
Noisy, Noisy & Quiet End Clusters in CVCC and CCVCC Words with Suffix *-s /s/*, *-s /z/* and *-es /əz/*

4. SENTENCE READING

The frog jumps on the fronds.

I can spot ants on the banks.

The camp has just six tents.

The skunks smell bad thanks to their glands.

Len spends a lot on his chimps.

My glasses have bad lenses.

Ben slumps at his desk, and his boss grants him a rest.

Thanks to that man, Bob has not got cramps in his legs.

Meg can spot the trends of all the brands.

The hog grunts as Ross tempts him to a bag of cobs.

5. SPELLING WORDS

jumps	sends	banks	helps	winks
stunts	grants	slumps	thanks	lenses

6. SENTENCE DICTATION

Rub the lenses with a cloth.

The banks lend lots of funds.

A frog jumps from the fronds to the sand banks.

The champs get all my thanks.

In ten winks, he spends a lot of cash.

EXAMPLE #32 LESSON PLAN FOR LEVEL 4
Digraph End Clusters with
Suffix *–es* in VCCC Words

Student/Class: Date: Lesson #:

1. ALPHABET CARD DRILL

Reading Drill

Show the student one **Alphabet Drill Card** at a time. The student writes/traces the letter saying the letter(s) name(s), keyword and sound.

Use **Teacher Prompts** if necessary.

What is the name of this letter?

What is the keyword?

What is the sound this letter makes?

For Multiple Spellings Teacher Asks	Student Answers
What are the two sounds s makes?	*s snake /s/, s nose /z/*
What are the two sounds c makes?	*c cat /k/, c dance /s/*
What are the two sounds g makes?	*g goat /g/, g hinge /j/*
What are the two sounds th makes?	*th thumb /th/, th there /th/*
What are the two sounds n makes?	*n net /n/ and n rink /ŋ/*

a	b	c and c₂	d	e	f
g and g₂	h	i	j	k	l
m	n and n₂	o	p	qu	r
s and s₂	t	u	v	w	x
y	z	ch	ck	sh	th and th₂
all	ng				

EXAMPLE #32 LESSON PLAN FOR LEVEL 4
Digraph End Clusters with
Suffix –es in VCCC Words

 Spelling Drill

Do not show student each **Alphabet Drill Card** and ask:

What letter spells the sounds?

The teacher says the sound and the student traces/writes the letter(s)while saying the letter name(s), keyword and sound.

For Multiple Spellings Teacher Asks	Student Answers
How many ways can you spell /k/?	*c, k, ck*
How many ways can you spell /z/?	*s, z*
How many ways can you spell /s/?	*c, s*
How many ways can you spell /j/?	*g, j*
How many ways can you spell /ŋ/?	*n, ng*

/ă/	/b/	/k/	/d/	/ĕ/	/f/
/g/	/h/	/ĭ/	/j/	/l/	/m/
/n/ and /ŋ/	/ŏ/	/p/	/kw/	/r/	/s/
/t/	/ŭ/	/v/	/w/	/ks/	/y/
/z/	/ch/	/sh/	/th/ and /th/	/awl/	

Suffix Drill

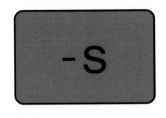 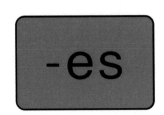

Teacher: *Please read the cards.*

Student: *–s says /s/ and /z/; -es says /əz/.*

Teacher: *What are the jobs of suffix –s and –es?*

Student: *They show plural (more than one), e.g. cats, kisses. They are used with he/she/it verbs, e.g. He digs. She sits. It yaps. He fishes. She rushes. It messes. Proper and common nouns can be used instead of he/she/it.*

2. BLENDING

b			
bl			
br			
cl	a		
cr		lch	
dr	e		s
f		nch	
g	i		
h		lth	
l	o		es
m		nth	
n	u		
p			
r			
st			
t			
tw			

3. WORD READING

blanch	belch	bench	winch	flinch
inch	filch	bunch	plinth	fifth
finch	gulch	hunch	filth	sixth
pinch	mulch	lunch	ranch	tenth
clinch	munch	punch	cinch	twelfth
French	brunch	blanch	zilch	width
stench	drench	stanch	winch	angst

SIGHT WORDS:

a	and	I
of	the	to
was	into	are
have	were	you
their	one	friend

4. SENTENCE READING

The man will clench his fist and punch the bag.

I will not flinch from a grim job.

It is a cinch to fix the winch.

Mick will munch on the cobs at the ranch.

Pick the nuts off the branch and blanch them.

That mulch has a bad stench.

I will have brunch with a French friend.

Ben will chat at length with Meg.

I had to add twelfths and fifths in my math test.

The benches are wet and have bunches of grass on them.

EXAMPLE #32 LESSON PLAN FOR LEVEL 4
Digraph End Clusters with
Suffix –es in VCCC Words

5. SPELLING WORDS

bunch	lunch	French	inch	belch
crunch	width	fifth	ranch	stench
inches	lunches	pinches	fifths	belches

6. SENTENCE DICTATION

That path runs the length of the dam.

Ten French men will have lunch on the ranch.

Jim belches if the lunches have yams.

Add the widths in inches.

The dress pinches at the neck.

EXAMPLE #33 LESSON PLAN FOR LEVEL 4
wh in CCVC & CCVCC Words

GREAT WORD HOUSE
Reading & Spelling Program

Student/Class: | **Date:** | **Lesson #:**

NEW CONCEPT: A digraph refers to two letters that make one sound. *wh* is a digraph only found at the beginning of words and is pronounced /w/. It can be introduced earlier as a Sight Word, such as, *what*.

Exceptions: *who, whom* and *whole, wh* sounds like /h/

1. ALPHABET CARD DRILL

Reading Drill

Show the student one **Alphabet Drill Card** at a time. The student writes/traces the letter saying the letter(s) name(s), keyword and sound.

Use **Teacher Prompts** if necessary.

What is the name of this letter?

What is the keyword?

What is the sound this letter makes?

For Multiple Spellings Teacher Asks	Student Answers
What are the two sounds s makes?	*s snake /s/, s nose /z/*
What are the two sounds c makes?	*c cat /k/, c dance /s/*
What are the two sounds g makes?	*g goat /g/, g hinge /j/*
What are the two sounds th makes?	*th thumb /th/, th there /th/*
What are the two sounds n makes?	*n net /n/ and n rink /ŋ/*

a	b	c and c₂	d	e	f
g and g₂	h	i	j	k	l
m	n and n₂	o	p	qu	r
s and s₂	t	u	v	w	x
y	z	ch	ck	sh	th and th₂
all	ng	wh			

EXAMPLE #33 LESSON PLAN FOR LEVEL 4
wh in CCVC & CCVCC Words

 Spelling Drill

Do not show student each **Alphabet Drill Card** and ask:

What letter spells the sounds?

The teacher says the sound and the student traces/writes the letter(s) while saying the letter name(s), keyword and sound.

For Multiple Spellings Teacher Asks	Student Answers
How many ways can you spell /k/?	*c, k, ck*
How many ways can you spell /z/?	*s, z*
How many ways can you spell /s/?	*c, s*
How many ways can you spell /j/?	*g, j*
How many ways can you spell /ŋ/?	*n, ng*
How many ways can you spell /w/?	*w, wh*

/ă/	/b/	/k/	/d/	/ĕ/	/f/
/g/	/h/	/ĭ/	/j/	/l/	/m/
/n/ and /ŋ/	/ŏ/	/p/	/kw/	/r/	/s/
/t/	/ŭ/	/v/	/w/	/ks/	/y/
/z/	/ch/	/sh/	/th/ and /th/	/awl/	

EXAMPLE #33 LESSON PLAN FOR LEVEL 4
wh in CCVC & CCVCC Words

2. BLENDING

wh	e i y	ch ff lk lp m n p sk st t zz

3. WORD READING

when	why	whisk
whelk	whim	whist
whelp	whip	which
whet	whit	whizz

SIGHT WORDS:

a	and	I
of	the	to
was	into	are
have	were	you
their	one	who
what	where	which

EXAMPLE #33 LESSON PLAN FOR LEVEL 4
wh in CCVC & CCVCC Words

4. SENTENCE READING

Where is my lunch tin?

What is in that box?

When will my dog get back from the vet?

Why is Ben in bed at ten?

Whisk that egg and mix in the nuts.

Crack that whip and get on with the job!

Which bench shall we sit on?

Where can I get a black silk dress?

Who is in the den with my cat?

On a whim, I went on a trip to France.

5. SPELLING WORDS

when	why	whisk	whim	whip
who	what	which	where	whose

6. SENTENCE DICTATION

When can I sit the math test?

Why is the prince not at the dance?

Who is that man with a red hat?

What is the width of the den?

Which clock is fast?

EXAMPLE #34 LESSON PLAN FOR LEVEL 4
Suffix *–ing* with Closed Syllable Words
Using No Spelling Rule, 111 Doubling Rule
and Drop the Silent e Rule

Student/Class: **Date:**   **Lesson #:**

NEW CONCEPT: Suffix *–ing* is a suffix that begins with a vowel. It is called a vowel suffix.

111 Doubling Rule: When a vowel suffix is added to a word that ends in one vowel and one consonant, the last consonant is doubled. This is called the **111 Doubling Spelling Rule**. See the **GWH Spelling Rule Book** for more information and exercises.

For example, *run + ing → running*

Exceptions: *w, x* do not double

Drop the e: When a vowel suffix is added to a word ending in a **Silent e**, then the **Silent e** is dropped. This is called the **Drop the e Spelling Rule**. See the **GWH Spelling Rule Book** for more information and exercises.

For example, *dance + ing → dancing*

EXAMPLE #34 LESSON PLAN FOR LEVEL 4
Suffix –ing with Closed Syllable Words Using No Spelling Rule, 111 Doubling Rule and Drop the Silent e Rule

1. ALPHABET CARD DRILL

Reading Drill

Show the student one **Alphabet Drill Card** at a time. The student writes/traces the letter saying the letter(s) name(s), keyword and sound.
Use **Teacher Prompts** if necessary.

What is the name of this letter?

What is the keyword?

What is the sound this letter makes?

For Multiple Spellings Teacher Asks	Student Answers
What are the two sounds s makes?	*s snake /s/, s nose /z/*
What are the two sounds c makes?	*c cat /k/, c dance /s/*
What are the two sounds g makes?	*g goat /g/, g hinge /j/*
What are the two sounds th makes?	*th thumb /th/, th there /th/*
What are the two sounds n makes?	*n net /n/ and n rink /ŋ/*

a	b	c and c$_2$	d	e	f
g and g$_2$	h	i	j	k	l
m	n and n$_2$	o	p	qu	r
s and s$_2$	t	u	v	w	x
y	z	ch	ck	sh	th and th$_2$
all	ng	wh			

EXAMPLE #34 LESSON PLAN FOR LEVEL 4
Suffix –*ing* with Closed Syllable Words Using No Spelling Rule, 111 Doubling Rule and Drop the Silent e Rule

Spelling Drill

Do not show student each **Alphabet Drill Card** and ask:

What letter spells the sounds?

The teacher says the sound and the student traces/writes the letter(s) while saying the letter name(s), keyword and sound.

For Multiple Spellings Teacher Asks	Student Answers
How many ways can you spell /k/?	c, k, ck
How many ways can you spell /z/?	s, z
How many ways can you spell /s/?	c, s
How many ways can you spell /j/?	g, j
How many ways can you spell /ŋ/?	n, ng

/ă/	/b/	/k/	/d/	/ĕ/	/f/
/g/	/h/	/ĭ/	/j/	/l/	/m/
/n/ and /ŋ/	/ŏ/	/p/	/kw/	/r/	/s/
/t/	/ŭ/	/v/	/w/	/ks/	/y/
/z/	/ch/	/sh/	/th/ and /<u>th</u>/	/awl/	

EXAMPLE #34 LESSON PLAN FOR LEVEL 4
Suffix *-ing* with Closed Syllable Words Using No Spelling Rule, 111 Doubling Rule and Drop the Silent e Rule

Suffix Drill

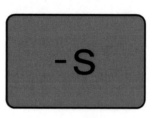 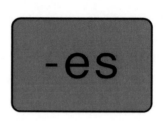 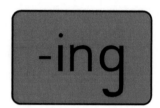

Teacher: *Please read the cards.*

Student: *–s says /s/ and /z/; -es says /əz/.*

Teacher: *What are the jobs of suffix –s and –es?*

Student: *They show plural (more than one), e.g. cats, kisses. They are used with he/she/it verbs, e.g. He digs. She sits. It yaps. He fishes. She rushes. It messes. Proper and common nouns can be used instead of he/she/it.*

Teacher: *What is job of suffix –ing?*

Student: *It is used with verbs, e.g. We are running. It forms nouns, e.g. padding.*

2. BLENDING

Include Word Wheels which are found in the Appendix: Drop e, 111 Doubling Rule, Just Add

Add *-ing* to the words below.

Drop e	Doubling Rule	Just Add
dance	clap	clasp
lunge	slog	fast
prance	shop	crest
bulge	clip	hand
whinge	rig	ask
wince	sit	twist
mince	cut	camp
chance	fan	send
fence	hem	plant
plunge	hug	risk
hinge	chop	end

GREAT
WORD
HOUSE
Reading & Spelling
Program

EXAMPLE #34 LESSON PLAN FOR LEVEL 4
Suffix –*ing* with Closed Syllable Words
Using No Spelling Rule, 111 Doubling Rule
and Drop the Silent e Rule

SCOPE & SEQUENCE
S
LEVELS 1-4

3. WORD READING

CVC 111 Rule	CCVC 111 Rule	CVCC No Rule	CCVCC/C No Rule	VCCe Drop e
matting	stunning	basking	twisting	lunging
running	clipping	acting	clasping	plunging
batting	shopping	risking	trusting	dancing
dimming	chipping	handing	shifting	wincing
sunning	blotting	mashing	chomping	mincing
hopping	dripping	wishing	shelling	bulging
tipping	plodding	buzzing	dressing	ranging
fanning	cramming	falling	flashing	fencing
winning	sledding	willing	trending	hinging
potting	shedding	masking	tempting	chancing
wedding	whipping	casting	belching	prancing
jetting	plugging	honking	munching	glancing

SIGHT WORDS:

a	and	I
of	the	to
was	into	are
have	were	you
their	one	who
what	where	which

Page 167

EXAMPLE #34 LESSON PLAN FOR LEVEL 4
Suffix *–ing* with Closed Syllable Words Using No Spelling Rule, 111 Doubling Rule and Drop the Silent e Rule

4. SENTENCE READING

They are jetting to the wedding in France.

Meg is sunning on the sand banks.

It is hot and the frog is jumping into the pond.

The bugs are buzzing and the ants are rushing.

Mick is in the cast and acting as the king.

The drops are dripping into the pan.

As the clock is ticking, the rat is sipping up the milk.

At six, the kids are dancing as they are dressing.

It is tempting to cash in my bonds and quit my job.

I am asking you to stop belching.

5. SPELLING WORDS

robbing	rubbing	bedding	shopping	clapping
chatting	asking	hanging	planting	bunching

6. SENTENCE DICTATION

The dogs are hopping and yapping.

Mom is trimming and hemming the dress.

Mick is acting well and they are clapping.

The ducks are quacking and munching on grass.

Dad is mixing up a hot pot.

EXAMPLE #35 LESSON PLAN FOR LEVEL 4
Suffix –ed with Closed Syllable Words
Using No Spelling Rule, 111 Doubling Rule
and Drop the Silent e Rule

SCOPE & SEQUENCE
S
LEVELS 4-1

Student/Class: Date: Lesson #:

NEW CONCEPT: The suffix -ed has three sounds /t/, /d/ and /ed/. When it sounds like /t/ and /d/, it may be confused with a part of the base word. Instruct the student to consider the part of speech of the word. If it is a past tense verb then the suffix –ed has been added.

-ed is a vowel suffix. When -ed is added to a word that ends in one vowel and one consonant, the last consonant is doubled. This is called the **111 Doubling Spelling Rule**. See the **GWH Spelling Rule Book** for more information and exercises.
For example, *fit + ed → fitted*

When a vowel suffix is added to a word ending in a **Silent e**, then the **Silent e** is dropped. This is called the **Drop the e Spelling Rule**. See the **GWH™ Spelling Rule Book** for more information and exercises.
For example, *dance + ed → danced*

EXAMPLE #35 LESSON PLAN FOR LEVEL 4
Suffix –*ed* with Closed Syllable Words Using No Spelling Rule, 111 Doubling Rule and Drop the Silent *e* Rule

1. ALPHABET CARD DRILL

Reading Drill

Show the student one **Alphabet Drill Card** at a time. The student writes/traces the letter saying the letter(s) name(s), keyword and sound.
Use **Teacher Prompts** if necessary.

What is the name of this letter?
What is the keyword?
What is the sound this letter makes?

For Multiple Spellings Teacher Asks	Student Answers
What are the two sounds s makes?	*s snake /s/, s nose /z/*
What are the two sounds c makes?	*c cat /k/, c dance /s/*
What are the two sounds g makes?	*g goat /g/, g hinge /j/*
What are the two sounds th makes?	*th thumb /th/, th there /th/*
What are the two sounds n makes?	*n net /n/ and n rink /ŋ/*

a	**b**	**c** and **c₂**	**d**	**e**	**f**
g and **g₂**	**h**	**i**	**j**	**k**	**l**
m	**n** and **n₂**	**o**	**p**	**qu**	**r**
s and **s₂**	**t**	**u**	**v**	**w**	**x**
y	**z**	**ch**	**ck**	**sh**	**th** and **th₂**
all	**ng**	**wh**			

EXAMPLE #35 LESSON PLAN FOR LEVEL 4
Suffix –ed with Closed Syllable Words Using No Spelling Rule, 111 Doubling Rule and Drop the Silent e Rule

Spelling Drill

Do not show student each **Alphabet Drill Card** and ask:

What letter spells the sounds?

The teacher says the sound and the student traces/writes the letter(s)while saying the letter name(s), keyword and sound.

For Multiple Spellings Teacher Asks	Student Answers
How many ways can you spell /k/?	c, k, ck
How many ways can you spell /z/?	s, z
How many ways can you spell /s/?	c, s
How many ways can you spell /j/?	g, j
How many ways can you spell /ŋ/?	n, ng

/ă/	/b/	/k/	/d/	/ĕ/	/f/
/g/	/h/	/ĭ/	/j/	/l/	/m/
/n/ and /ŋ/	/ŏ/	/p/	/kw/	/r/	/s/
/t/	/ŭ/	/v/	/w/	/ks/	/y/
/z/	/ch/	/sh/	/th/ and /th/	/awl/	

EXAMPLE #35 LESSON PLAN FOR LEVEL 4
Suffix –*ed* with Closed Syllable Words Using No Spelling Rule, 111 Doubling Rule and Drop the Silent *e* Rule

Suffix Drill

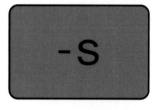   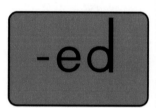

Teacher: *Please read the cards.*

Student: *–s says /s/ and /z/; -es says /əz/.*

Teacher: *What are the jobs of suffix –s and –es?*

Student: *They show plural (more than one), e.g. cats, kisses. They are used with he/she/it verbs, e.g. He digs. She sits. It yaps He fishes. She rushes. It messes. Proper and common nouns can be used instead of he/she/it.*

Teacher: *What is job of suffix –ing?*

Student: *It is used with verbs, e.g. We are running. It forms nouns, e.g. padding.*

Teacher: *What is the job of suffix –ed?*

Student: *It is used to show the past tense form of the verb.*

EXAMPLE #35 LESSON PLAN FOR LEVEL 4
Suffix –*ed* with Closed Syllable Words Using No Spelling Rule, 111 Doubling Rule and Drop the Silent *e* Rule

SCOPE & SEQUENCE
LEVELS 1-4
S

2. BLENDING

Include **Word Wheels** found in the Appendix: Drop e, 111 Doubling Rule, Just Add

Add -*ed* to the words below.

Drop e	Doubling Rule	No Rule
dance	clap	clasp
lunge	slog	last
prance	shop	crest
bulge	clip	land
whinge	rig	ask
wince	fix	twist
mince	sip	camp
chance	fan	fill
fence	hem	plant
plunge	hug	risk
hinge	chop	end

EXAMPLE #35 LESSON PLAN FOR LEVEL 4
Suffix –*ed* with Closed Syllable Words Using No Spelling Rule, 111 Doubling Rule and Drop the Silent *e* Rule

3. WORD READING

No Spelling Rule		
ed /t/	**ed /d/**	**ed /əd/**
asked	filled	acted
fussed	buzzed	opted
kissed	billed	landed
wished	filmed	tinted
basked	spelled	dented
banked	killed	nested
gasped	stalled	added
licked	grilled	hinted
honked	felled	rested
risked	winged	gusted
messed	hanged	mended
wished	ringed	printed
bathed	longed	slanted
pressed	stringed	trusted
dressed	shelled	chanted
crushed	spilled	drifted
smashed	velled	shifted

EXAMPLE #35 LESSON PLAN FOR LEVEL 4
Suffix –*ed* with Closed Syllable Words
Using No Spelling Rule, 111 Doubling Rule
and Drop the Silent *e* Rule

111 Doubling Rule		
ed /t/	ed /d/	ed /əd/
hopped	hummed	batted
sipped	dimmed	fitted
slipped	sunned	dotted
whipped	lugged	jetted
stopped	logged	pitted
lapped	buzzed	wedded
mopped	stunned	chatted
clipped	crammed	plodded
dripped	slogged	thudded
clapped	plugged	chatted

Drop e Rule		
ed /t/	ed /d/	ed /əd/
winced	singed	*
minced	tinged	
danced	bulged	
fenced	ranged	
lanced	plunged	
chanced	lunged	
pranced	hinged	
glanced	cringed	

*no words at this level

GREAT WORD HOUSE
Reading & Spelling Program

EXAMPLE #35 LESSON PLAN FOR LEVEL 4
Suffix –*ed* with Closed Syllable Words Using No Spelling Rule, 111 Doubling Rule and Drop the Silent *e* Rule

SIGHT WORDS:

a	and	I
of	the	to
was	into	are
have	were	you
who	what	where
which	one	their

4. SENTENCE READING

əd /əd/ No Spelling Rule

I handed in one of my bags.

The boss hinted that I did well.

A finch nested in the branch.

My glasses are tinted to block the sun.

The winds gusted and I opted to get on a bus.

ed /əd/ 111 Doubling Rule

The rug is matted with mud.

The dress is dotted with red spots.

Gus jetted off on a trip to France.

That black bug is six-legged.

Jack has had a long spell of wedded bliss.

EXAMPLE #35 LESSON PLAN FOR LEVEL 4
Suffix *–ed* with Closed Syllable Words Using No Spelling Rule, 111 Doubling Rule and Drop the Silent *e* Rule

əd /d/ No Spelling Rule

Ken filmed the fun trip.

Pam spilled the milk on the mat.

The bug buzzed on the jam lid.

Ben spelled the best on the test.

The pop fizzed in the mug.

ed /d/ 111 Doubling Rule

Ned scanned the ship for canned fish.

Len bragged that he did best.

The boss shrugged off the lost cash.

Dan pinned up the hem.

Seth gabbed on and on.

ed /d/ Drop e Rule

Jan lunged at Jim in fencing class.

His tum bulged from all the pop he had drunk.

The sack bulged with lots of rags.

A lot hinged on fixing the van fast.

At dusk, the sky is tinged pink.

EXAMPLE #35 LESSON PLAN FOR LEVEL 4
Suffix –*ed* with Closed Syllable Words Using No Spelling Rule, 111 Doubling Rule and Drop the Silent *e* Rule

əd /t/ No Spelling Rule

The clock clanked and clicked.

Len bashed his chin as he ran.

The math stumped the class.

I dashed to chess club.

Mick lacked cash and had to get a job.

ed /t/ 111 Doubling Rule

A frog hopped to the pond.

The bus stopped and the kids got off.

We fixed the tap that dripped.

The cat lapped up the milk.

They clapped when Tom did a jig.

ed /t/ Drop *e* Rule

The prince pranced at the dance.

The path was fenced with rocks and planks.

Gus winced when he bit his lip.

Mom minced the fish for lunch.

The vet lanced the big spot.

GREAT WORD HOUSE
Reading & Spelling Program

EXAMPLE #35 LESSON PLAN FOR LEVEL 4
Suffix *-ed* with Closed Syllable Words Using No Spelling Rule, 111 Doubling Rule and Drop the Silent *e* Rule

SCOPE & SEQUENCE
S
LEVELS 4-1

5. SPELLING WORDS

	ed /t/	ed /d/	ed /əd/
No Rule	licked	filled	rested
Doubling Rule	hopped	manned	potted
Drop e Rule	danced	bulged	*

6. SENTENCE DICTATION

My glasses are tinted.

The brush is matted with mud.

I filled my cup with milk.

Tom hummed as he did his job.

The cat got mad and lunged.

Mick locked up the hut.

The mast snapped and the ship tipped.

Len danced all the jigs with Nan.

GREAT
WORD
HOUSE

**Reading & Spelling
Program**

APPENDIX

Terminology
Levels 1 - 4

Terminology

Establish a common terminology with your student. Ensure that your student understands all the terminology that you will use. The student needs to provide a definition of each term and demonstrate this knowledge. Teach terminology on a "needs to know" basis.

Base Word

A stem originating from the Anglo-Saxon or Old English period is referred to as a base word. Anglo-Saxon base words are the oldest words in our language and originate from what is now known as Germany, Holland and Denmark. Base words have the most accessible meanings: they are words used for everyday life, family relationships, basic colours, numbers to 1000 and are the first words learned. High Frequency and Sight Words are mostly Anglo-Saxon. They have words with -*ck*, -*tch*, -*dge*, digraphs, double letters, silent letters and vowel teams. No *j* in Anglo-Saxon base words.

Suffix

A suffix is attached after the stem, changes the part of speech and sometimes the meaning. A vowel suffix begins with a vowel, e.g. -*ed*. A consonant suffix begins with a consonant, e.g. -*s*.

FF-LL-SS-ZZ Rule

At the end of a short word, after a short vowel sound, double the *f*, *l*, *s*, and *z*.

Drop the Silent e Rule

When a vowel suffix is added to a word ending in a Silent e, then the Silent e is dropped.

111 Doubling Rule

In a one-syllable word, ending in one vowel and one consonant, double final consonant when adding a vowel suffix.

SPELLING WORDS

Listen

Repeat

Sound out

Say letter names

Write and say letter names

Read back

SENTENCE DICTATION

1. Listen.

2. Repeat.

3. Write down.

4. Check for capitals.

5. Check for periods.

Lesson Template

Sentence Dictation Template

WORD FAMILIES

short a	short i	short e	short o	short u
at	**it**	**et**	**ot**	**ut**
bat	bit	bet	bot	but
cat	fit	get	cot	cut
fat	hit	jet	dot	gut
hat	kit	let	got	hut
mat	lit	met	hot	jut
Nat	mit	net	jot	nit
pat	nit	pet	lot	put
rat	pit	set	not	rut
sat	sit	vet	pot	Tut
tat	wit	wet	rot	vat
	zit	yet	tot	
ab	**ib**	**eb**	**ob**	**ub**
cab	bib	Deb	bob	bub
dab	dib	Feb.	cob	cub
fab	fib	web	dob	dub
gab	gib		fob	hub
jab	jib		gob	nub
lab	lib		hob	pub
nab	nib		job	rub
tab	rib		lob	tub
			mob	
ad	**id**	**ed**	nob	
bad	bid	bed	rob	
cad	did	fed	sob	
dad	hid	led	yob	
fad	lid	Ned		
gad	rid	red	**od**	**ud**
lad		wed	cod	cud
mad		zed	god	dud
pad			mod	mud
rad			nod	
sad			pod	
tad			rod	

WORD FAMILIES

short a	short i	short e	short o	short u
			sod	
an	**in**	**en**	tod	**un**
ban	bin	Ben		bun
can	din	den	**on**	dun
Dan	fin	fen	bon	gun
fan	gin	hen	con	fun
man	pin	men	don	nun
nan	sin	pen	non	pun
pan	tin	ten	ton	run
ran	win	wen	son	sun
tan		yen	won	
van		Zen	yon	
ap	**ip**	**ep**	**op**	**up**
bap	dip	pep	bop	cup
cap	hip	rep.	cop	pup
gap	kip	yep	fop	sup
lap	lip		hop	yup
map	nip		lop	
nap	pip		mop	
rap	rip		pop	
sap	sip		sop	
zap	zip			
ag	**ig**	**eg**	**og**	**ug**
bag	big	beg	bog	bug
gag	dig	leg	cog	dug
hag	fig	peg	dog	hug
lag	gig		fog	lug
mag	pig		Gog	mug
nag	rig		hog	pug
rag	wig		log	rug
sag	zip		mog	tug
tag			nog	
wag			pog	

WORD FAMILIES

short a	short i	short e	short o	short u
zag			tog	
			jog	
am	**im**	**em**	**om**	**um**
cam	dim	gem	com-	bum
dam	him	hem	-dom	gum
ham	Jim	mem	hom	hum
jam	Kim		mom	mum
lam	Mim		nom	rum
Pam	rim		Pom	sum
ram	Sim		Tom	tum
Sam	Tim			yum
	Vim			
ax	**ix**	**ex**	**ox**	**ux**
fax	fix	hex	box	lux
lax	mix	sex	cox	tux
pax	nix	Tex	fox	
Max	pix	vex	lox	
sax	six		pox	
tax			sox	
wax			tox	
			vox	
Al		**el**		**us**
Cal		gel		bus
gal				pus
Hal				
pal				
Sal				
Val				

Sight Words

a

the

to

of

in

and

is

you	for
it	be
he	this
was	have

from	on
one	are
she	as
her	with

his

they

I

at

Word Families

am

ab

an

ad

ap

ag

at

all	ig
ass	im
ib	in
id	ip

it	eg
ix	em
eb	en
ed	ep

et	ob
ex	od
ess	og
ell	om

on	off
op	oss
ot	ub
ox	ud

ug	us
um	ut
un	ux
up	uff

ull

uss

uzz

BINGO

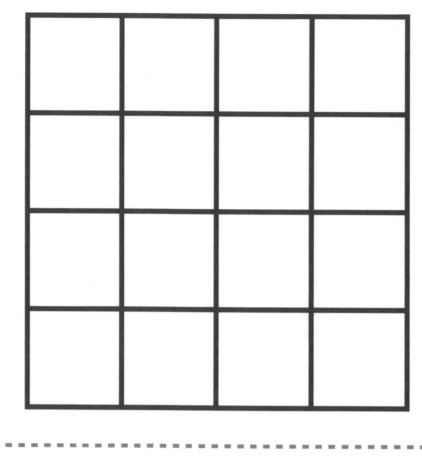

BINGO

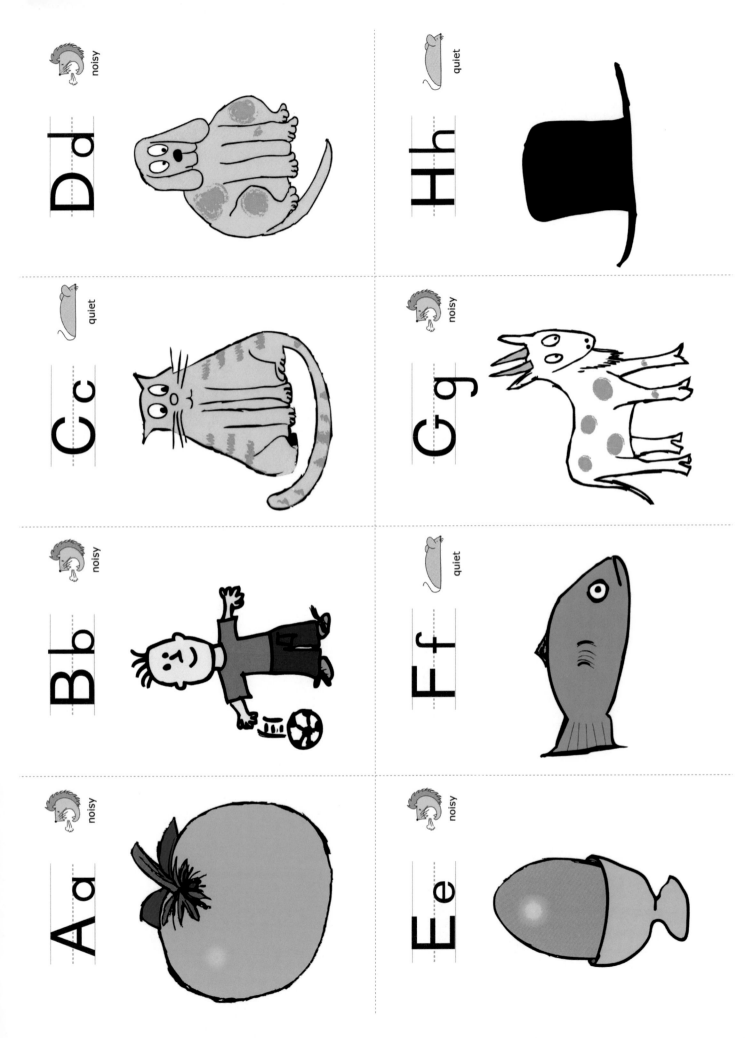

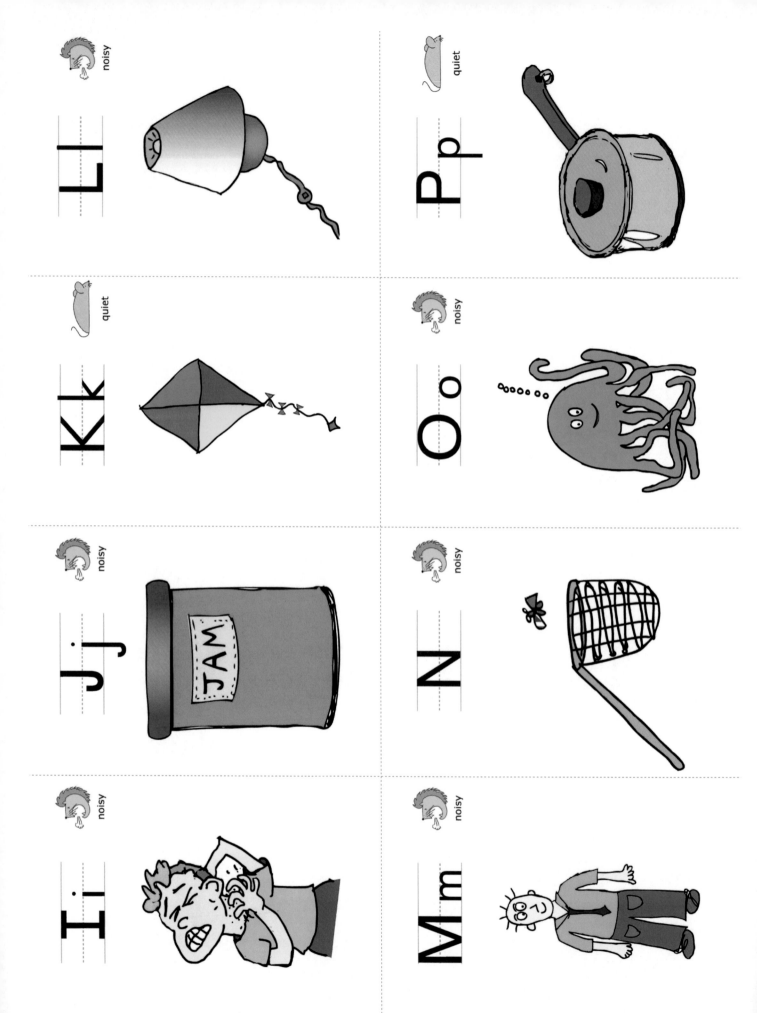

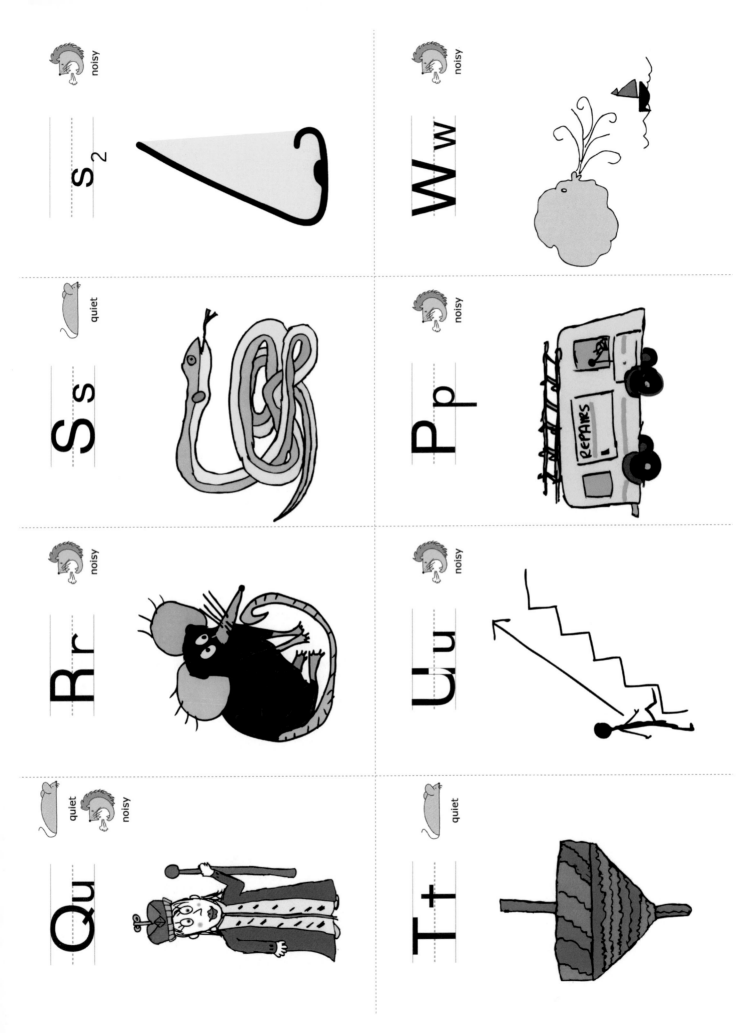

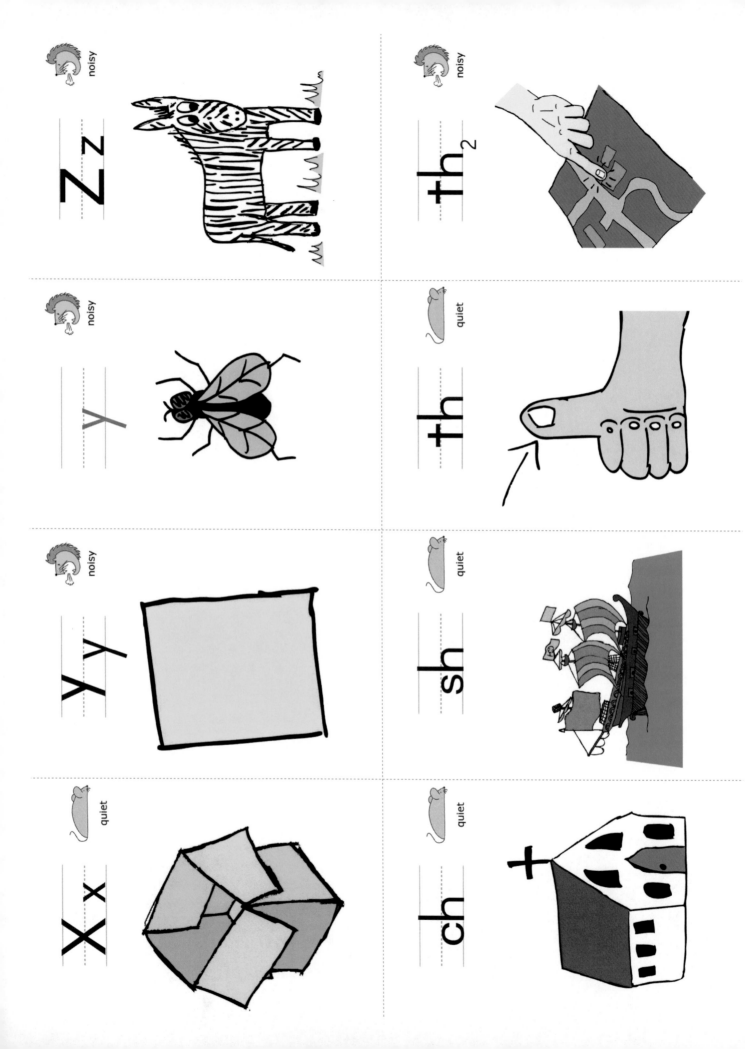

Zz noisy

Y noisy

Yy noisy

Xx quiet

th₂ noisy

th quiet

sh quiet

ch quiet

Noisy Letters

Noisy letters vibrate the vocal cords or voice box. All vowels are noisy and some consonants and digraphs are noisy.

Vowels

A vowel is a noisy stream of unblocked air. Vowels can say their names. Every word must have a vowel sound and a vowel letter.

a
e
i
o
u
y

Digraphs

A digraph is two letters that make one sound.

-ck
ch
sh
th
wh-

quiet

-ck

Quiet Letters

Quiet letters do not vibrate the vocal cords or voice box. Some consonants and digraphs are quiet.

Consonants

Consonants have some part of the mouth blocking the free flow of air. Consonants can be quiet or noisy.

b c d f g h j
k l m n p q r
s t v w x y z

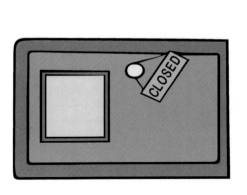

OPEN

CLOSED

Initial
Clusters/Digraphs
with Pictures

br-

brush

bl-

block

ch-

chair

bl-

blanket

ch-

church

br-

broom

cl-

clock

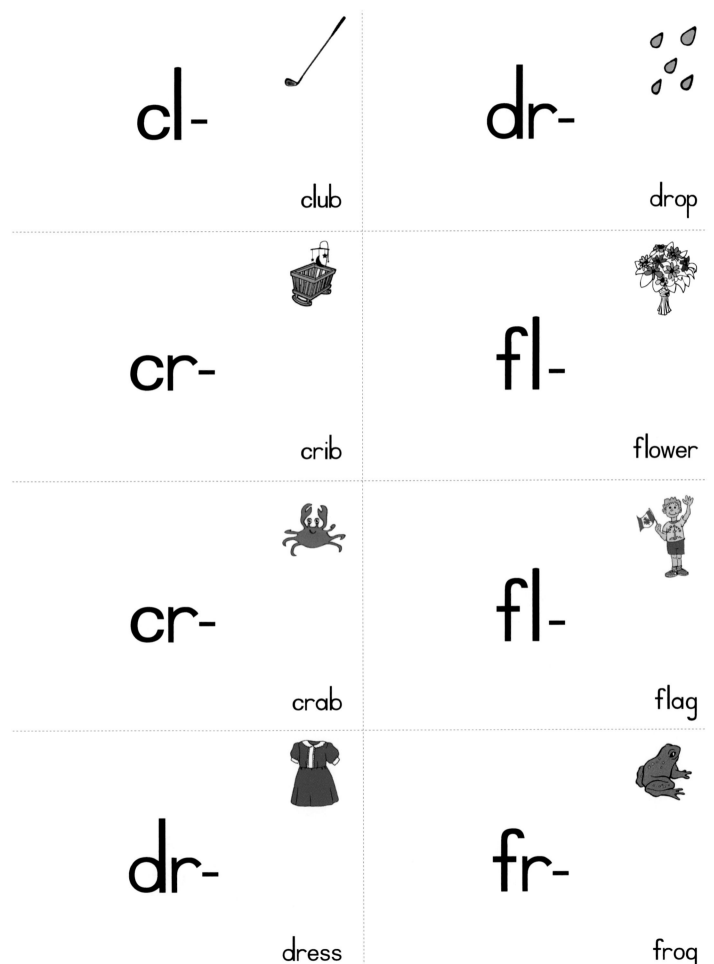

cl-   club

dr-   drop

cr-   crib

fl-   flower

cr-   crab

fl-   flag

dr-   dress

fr-   frog

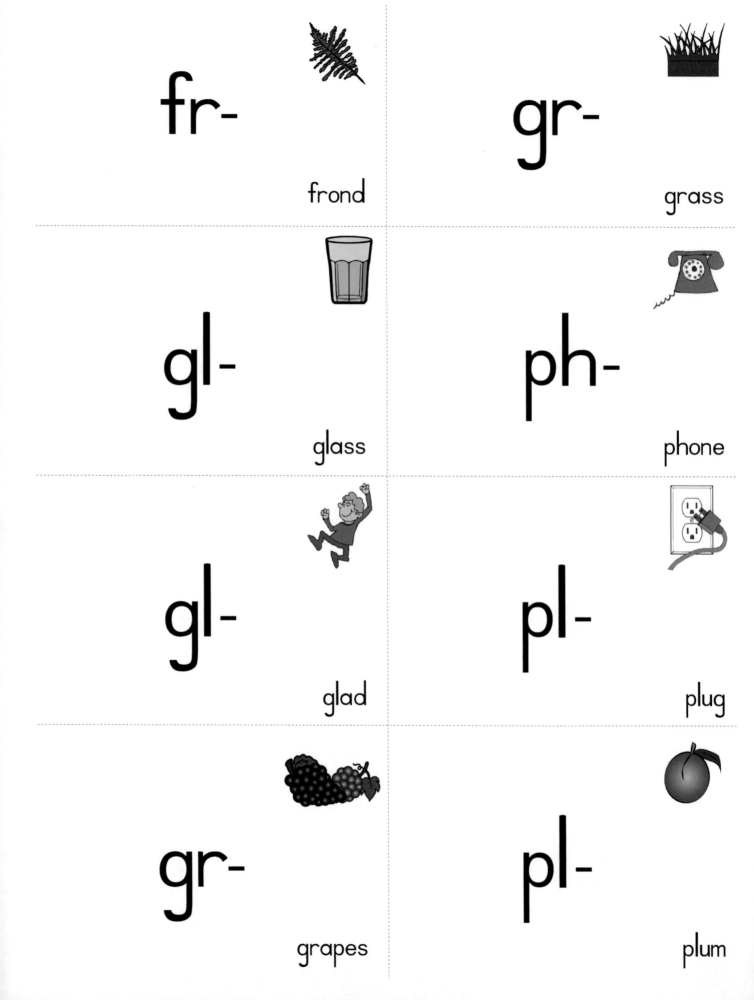

fr-

frond

gr-

grass

gl-

glass

ph-

phone

gl-

glad

pl-

plug

gr-

grapes

pl-

plum

pr-

present

pr-

prize

sc-

scarecrow

sc-

scale

scr-

scrub

scr-

scratch

sh-

shoe

sh-

ship

shr-

shrug

sl-

slide

shr-

shrimp

sl-

sled

sk-

skate

sm-

smoke

sk-

skip

sm-

smell

sn-

snail

spl-

splash

sn-

snack

spl-

split

sp-

spill

spr-

spring

sp-

spider

spr-

sprinkler

squ-

square

str-

strap

squ-

squish

str-

strawberry

st-

stop

sw-

swing

st-

stamp

sw-

sweater

th-

thumb

thr-

three

th-

there

thr-

thread

th-

thin

tr-

train

th-

the

tr-

tree

tw-

tweet

tw-

twins

wh-

whale

wh-

whip

Final
Clusters/Digraphs
with Pictures

-ft

lift

-ang

bang

-ing

ring

-ck

duck

-ink

sink

-ct

act

-ld

weld

-lf

golf

-mp

lamp

-lk

milk

-nch

bench

-lp

help

-nd

wind

-lt

belt

-nt

tent

-ong

song

-pt

slept

-sk

desk

-sp

wasp

-st

nest

-tch

catch

-ung

swung

-sh

fish

-ch

church

-unk

sunk

-th

math

-onk

honk

-dge

judge

-lm

film

-ank

bank

-lch

mulch

-nth

tenth

-nce

dance

-lth

wealth

-nge

hinge

-nk

sink

-ng

ring

Suffixes

-ed

-s

-ed

-s

-ed

-es

-ing

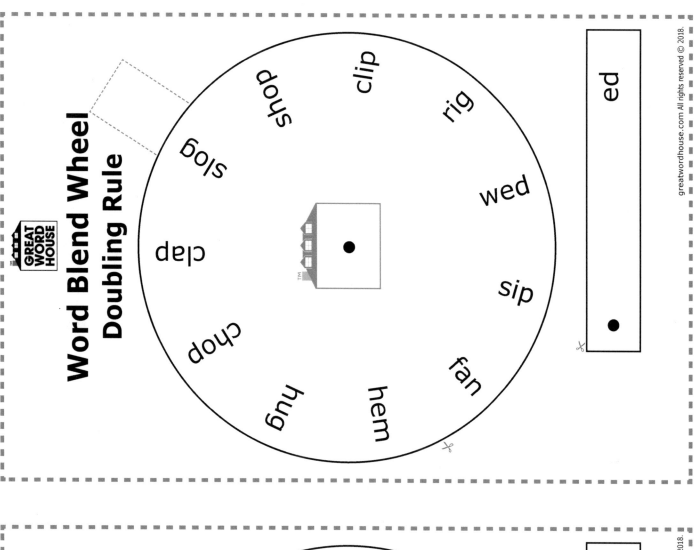

Word Blend Wheel
Doubling Rule

ed

clip
rig
wed
sip
fan
hem
hug
chop
clap
slog
shop

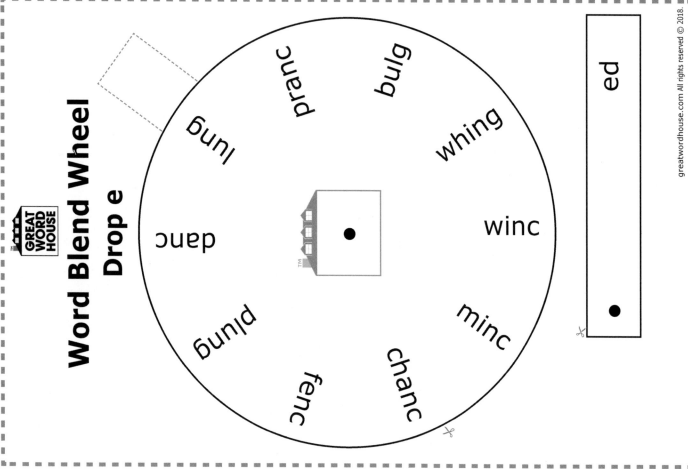

Word Blend Wheel
Drop e

ed

pranc
bulg
whing
winc
minc
chanc
fenc
plung
danc
lung

Word Blend Wheel
Blank

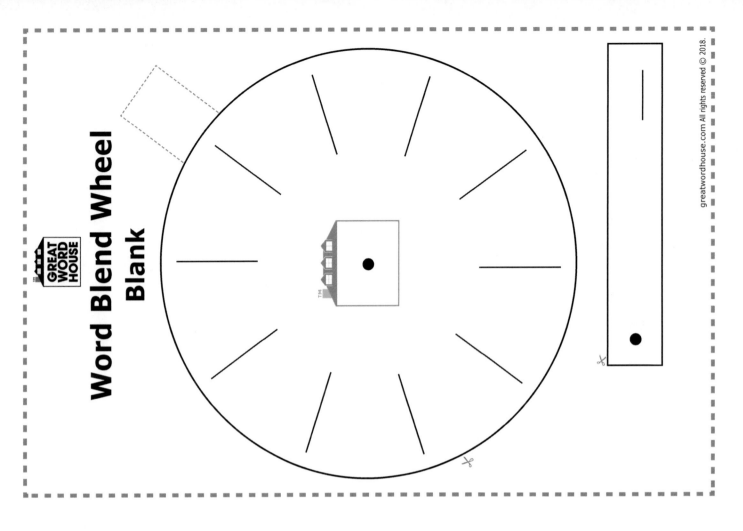

Word Blend Wheel
No Rule

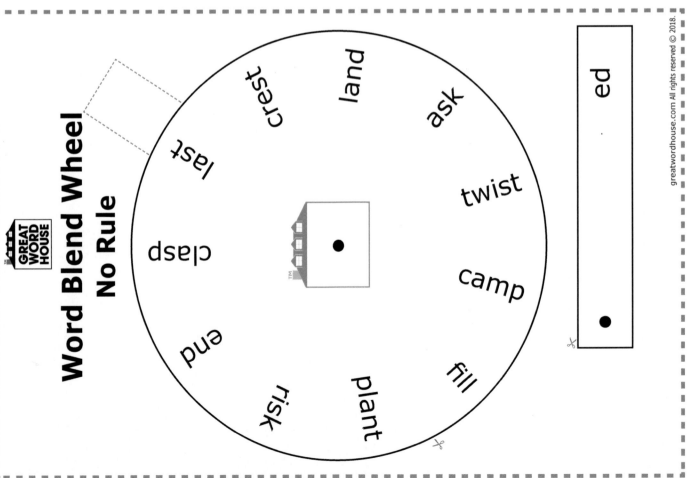

ed

TACHISTOSCOPE

Using this simple tachistoscope, the teacher can present the student with a variety of words to read and copy out. Each time a strip slides to show a different letter, a different word is created. The tachistoscope can be used to create real words for reading and spelling, and non-words for reading only. Print out the templates on card stock. Cut strips and slide through the slits indicated. Build words using single letters, digraphs, word families, prefixes and suffixes.

Slide strip through the slot.

b
c
d
f
h
t

Slide strip through the slot.

o

Slide strip through the slot.

g
m
n
t

TACHISTOSCOPE

Using this simple tachistoscope, the teacher can present the student with a variety of words to read and copy out. Each time a strip slides to show a different letter, a different word is created. The tachistoscope can be used to create real words for reading and spelling, and non-words for reading only. Print out the templates on card stock. Cut strips and slide through the slits indicated. Build words using single letters, digraphs, word families, prefixes and suffixes.

Slide strip through the slot.

Slide strip through the slot.

Slide strip through the slot.

TACHISTOSCOPE

✂ - - - - - - - - - - - - - - -   ✂ - - - - - - - - - - - - - - -

✂ - - - - - - - - - - - - - - -   ✂ - - - - - - - - - - - - - - -

TACHISTOSCOPE

LEVEL 1

SCOPE & SEQUENCE

This certificate is awarded to

Student Name

for the successful completion of

Great Word House™

Scope & Sequence Level 1

Teacher Name

Date

™

GREAT
WORD
HOUSE

LEVEL 2
SCOPE & SEQUENCE

This certificate is awarded to

_____

Student Name

for the successful completion of

Great Word House™

Scope & Sequence Level 2

_____

Teacher Name

_____

Date

GREAT WORD HOUSE ™

LEVEL
3
SCOPE & SEQUENCE

This certificate is awarded to

Student Name

for the successful completion of

Great Word House™

Scope & Sequence Level 3

Date

GREAT WORD HOUSE
™

Teacher Name

GREAT WORD HOUSE

LEVEL **4**
SCOPE & SEQUENCE

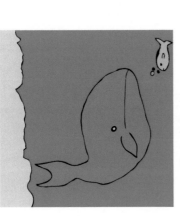

This certificate is awarded to

_____

Student Name

for the successful completion of

Great Word House™

Scope & Sequence Level 4

_____

Date

_____

Teacher Name